Rostov-on-Don and Kharkov 1942–43

Waffen-SS Soldier

VERSUS

Soviet Rifleman

Chris McNab

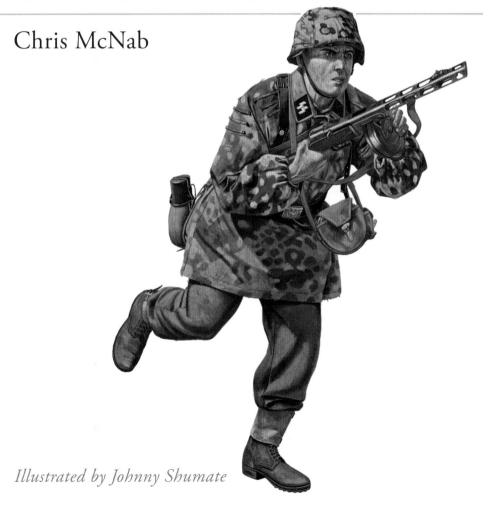

Illustrated by Johnny Shumate

OSPREY PUBLISHING
Bloomsbury Publishing Plc
Kemp House, Chawley Park, Cumnor Hill, Oxford OX2 9PH, UK
29 Earlsfort Terrace, Dublin 2, Ireland
1385 Broadway, 5th Floor, New York, NY 10018, USA
E-mail: info@ospreypublishing.com
www.ospreypublishing.com

OSPREY is a trademark of Osprey Publishing Ltd

First published in Great Britain in 2023

A catalogue record for this book is available from the British Library.

ISBN: PB 9781472857989; eBook 9781472857972;
ePDF 9781472858009; XML 9781472857996

23 24 25 26 27   10 9 8 7 6 5 4 3 2 1

Maps by www.bounford.com
Index by Rob Munro
Typeset by PDQ Digital Media Solutions, Bungay, UK
Printed and bound in India by Replika Press Private Ltd.

Osprey Publishing supports the Woodland Trust, the UK's leading
woodland conservation charity.

To find out more about our authors and books visit
www.ospreypublishing.com. Here you will find extracts, author
interviews, details of forthcoming events and the option to sign up for
our newsletter.

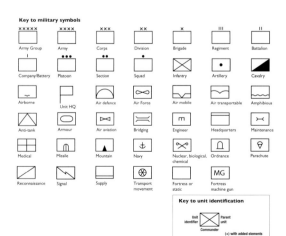

CONTENTS

Introduction

Kharkov in ruins in the middle years of the Great Patriotic War. (AirSeaLand/Cody Images)

On 22 June 1941, some 3.8 million Axis military personnel, along with more than 6,500 tanks and other armoured fighting vehicles, 600,000 motor vehicles, 600,000 horses, tens of thousands of artillery pieces and mortars and more than 3,000 combat aircraft surged across the borders of the Soviet Union. It was a wave of steel and fire the likes of which history had never witnessed. It was also, of course, the beginning of Operation *Barbarossa*,

Hitler's hubristic gamble to achieve the *Lebensraum* ('living space') that he saw as the teleological, geographical and racial destiny of the German people.

Within the mass of the Operation *Barbarossa* movement were a handful of divisions and regiments from the Waffen-SS (Armed SS). The *Schutzstaffel* (SS; Protection Squads) umbrella under which the Waffen-SS fell began life as a small bodyguard force around emerging political rebel Adolf Hitler and the nascent Nationalsozialistische Deutsche Arbeiterpartei (NSDAP; National Socialist German Workers' Party) in the mid-1920s, but by 1941 – and especially under the leadership of Reichsführer-SS Heinrich Himmler – it had become a virtual state within a state. The SS was a fanatically aligned instrument of Nazi power and control, with effective domination over the police and intelligence services, running a growing business empire through its control of the concentration camps, and increasingly providing an elite combat arm, the Waffen-SS. The Waffen-SS (it actually acquired the name in 1940) consequently became distinguished from the Allgemeine-SS (General-SS), which was composed of the administrative, security and concentration-camp branches of the SS.

By the time of Operation *Barbarossa*, the combat elements of the SS had already seen action in Poland in 1939, France and the Netherlands in 1940 and the Balkans in 1941. These early actions began forging the Waffen-SS's formidable reputation for combat daring and Nazi loyalty, with regimental or divisional honorifics such as *Leibstandarte SS Adolf Hitler* (*LSSAH*), *Totenkopf*, *Wiking*, *Deutschland*, *Germania* and *Der Führer* being trumpeted loud in Nazi propaganda while earning an inverse notoriety among the Allies – acts of massacre and indiscriminate cruelty eventually became intrinsic to the SS 'brand', although the culpability for war atrocities could vary considerably

Waffen-SS troops engage in street fighting on the Eastern Front. Note the very light amounts of equipment they carry with them into battle; they would generally leave heavier packs in rear areas or on vehicles, focusing mainly on weapons and ammunition. (AirSeaLand/Cody Images)

according to unit and commander. From mid-1941 onwards, however, it was the war on the Eastern Front that became, in a sense, the arena in which the Waffen-SS was truly destined to fight; the theatre in which Hitler's grotesque, titanic view of racial and ideological struggle would play out on its greatest scale.

The Waffen-SS was a rather marginal component of Operation *Barbarossa*, certainly compared to the mighty Heer (Army). The Oberkommando der Werhmacht (OKW; High Command of the Armed Forces) allocated almost 150 divisions to the invasion of the Soviet Union, but of these the Waffen-SS contributed only six divisions, one motorized regiment (*LSSAH*, which became a full division in July 1942) and three independent brigades. The Waffen-SS, however, was destined to grow massively during the remaining years of World War II, so that by the end of the conflict *c*.900,000 men had served in its ranks in 38 divisions. This figure was still a drop in the ocean compared to the 13 million soldiers who passed through the ranks of the wartime Heer (although it should be noted that the Waffen-SS Panzer divisions eventually constituted 25 per cent of the Wehrmacht's tank strength), but the Waffen-SS had an impact beyond its numbers. Its ideological drive, rigorous training, combat skills and elite status meant that it was often at the forefront of major offensive and defensive battles, as we shall see in the great street and field battles in and around Rostov-on-Don and Kharkov in 1942–43. As the tide of war turned against Germany, Waffen-SS formations were often famously deployed in 'fire-fighter' roles, rushed to parts of the front where dependably obdurate resistance or tactical flair was needed. In this context, the Waffen-SS's

official commitment to 'obedience unto death' was fully tested, especially as its ranks were progressively opened up to non-German membership (see 'The Opposing Sides').

On the Eastern Front, the Waffen-SS *Panzergrenadiere* (the principal focus of this study) came up against a very different type of enemy: the Soviet rifleman. The Waffen-SS forged its reputation partly on prowess and elite exclusivity. The Soviet riflemen, by contrast, were primarily about *mass*. The Soviet rifleman was a single drop in a mostly conscript sea, often inadequately trained and equipped, sometimes poorly led, tactically governed by a centralized command structure rather than the Waffen-SS's modern emphasis on devolved small-unit initiative. We can make, and support, a general claim that the Waffen-SS *Panzergrenadiere* were the superior soldiers *tactically* on a man-for-man basis, at least in terms of professional skills. We can also recognize that Stalin's axiom 'Quantity has a quality of its own' had a profound ring of truth on the Eastern Front. It is not right, however, to present the Soviet rifleman as nothing more than a crude battering-ram in a numbers game. Like his Waffen-SS opponent, he often had a thick seam of ideological indoctrination running through his character, reinforced by the compelling motivation that each soldier was fighting for his own country. His tactical skills, from individual to formation levels, also grew with experience and with some eventual doctrinal shifts. By 1942–43, the soldiers of the Waffen-SS might still have been ideologically contemptuous of their enemy, but they could no longer dismiss his fighting abilities.

Armour and infantry of the SS-Panzerkorps advance into Kharkov in early 1943, the tank commanders making careful study of the ground ahead of them. Waffen-SS tank commanders were encouraged to stand up in their open turret hatches during attacks to achieve better battlefield awareness – a policy that resulted in heavy casualties. (AirSeaLand/Cody Images)

The purpose behind *Fall Blau* (*Case Blue*) was to make a deep penetration in the south of the Soviet Union, occupying a defensive line along the Don River from Voronezh to the bend of the Volga River at Stalingrad, and swing down into the northern Caucasus to capture its extensive oilfields. This great sweep would be performed by two Axis army groups: Heeresgruppe B as the northern arm heading for Stalingrad – portentously, Hitler subsequently decided that the army group had to capture Stalingrad itself – and Heeresgruppe A making the swinging drive south into the Caucasus.

Fall Blau was launched on 28 June 1942. For a time, it brought back memories of the euphoric German advances of 1941. Heeresgruppe B would reach Stalingrad by September 1942, there to begin what is surely the greatest city battle in history, while Heeresgruppe A pushed some 500km into the Caucasus, taking many of the desired oilfields. As history reveals, however, there were deep fault lines in Hitler's core plan and also in his decision, on 17 July, to divert the 4. Panzerarmee from the push on Stalingrad to assist Heeresgruppe A's southerly advance along the Don River – a decision that slowed and weakened the northern advance on Stalingrad, and set the scene for a future catastrophe for the Axis. Furthermore, ferocious resistance by the Soviet Caucasus Front and the Trans-Caucasus Front meant that although Heeresgruppe A had advanced 500km into the Caucasus by November, it still fell short of the Batumi–Baku line that was the original objective.

This image of Soviet infantrymen on the march shows kit and equipment to good effect. Note how many of the men have their *plasch-palatka* cape/shelter-half carried in the traditional way – rolled up and hung over one shoulder, with the opposite ends tied at the hip to form a horseshoe shape. (AirSeaLand/Cody Images)

In this book, we will explore examples in which the Waffen-SS and the Red Army rifleman clashed in combat, and what those instances say about their respective approaches to making war. The focus is upon the operations of 1942–43, specifically to three actions from the battle for Rostov-on-Don in July 1942 through to what is now called the Fourth Battle of Kharkov in August 1943. During this period, the ultimate outcome of World War II hung in the balance. Illusions of German supremacy had been dispelled by defeats such as those at Stalingrad and Kursk, but the capacity of the Red Army to drive all the way through to Germany by no means seemed inevitable. The two sides in these battles could not have been more different; what they shared was their unwavering commitment to victory.

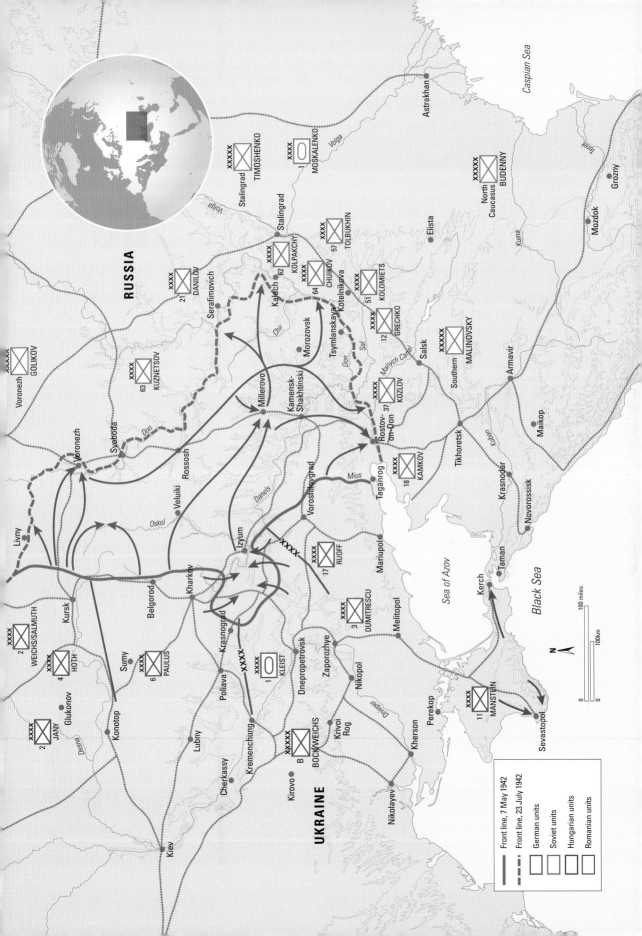

Caspian Sea

RUSSIA

Astrakhan

Grozny

Mozdok

Elista

Maikop

Armavir

Kuma

Terek

Volga

XXXXX TIMOSHENKO
Stalingrad

XXXX 1 MOSKALENKO

XXXXX North Caucasus BUDENNY

XXXX 21 DANILOV
Serafimovich

XXXX 62 KOLPAKCHI
Stalingrad

XXXX 57 TOLBUKHIN

XXXX 64 CHUIKOV
Kalach

XXXX 51 Kotelnikova KOLOMIETS

XXXX 63 KUZNETSOV

XXXX 12 GRECHKO

Salsk

Chir

Morozovsk

Tsymlanskaya

Sal

Don

Manych Canal

XXXX 37 KOZLOV

Tikhoretsk

Krasnodar

Novorossisk

Taman

Kerch

Kuban

XXXXX Southern MALINOVSKY

XXXXX GOLIKOV
Voronezh

Svoboda

Don

Millerovo

Kamensk-Shakhtinski

Rostov-on-Don

XXXX 18 KAMKOV
Taganrog

Mius

Rossosh

Oskol

Veluiki

Danels

Voroshilovgrad

Mariupol

Sea of Azov

Black Sea

Livny

Voronezh

Izyum

XXXX 17 RUOFF

Kharkov

Belgorod

Krasnograd

XXXX 3 DUMITRESCU

Melitopol

Nikopol

Dnepropetrovsk

Zaporozhye

Kherson

Perekop

Sevastopol

XXXX 11 MANSTEIN

XXXX 2 WEICHS/SALMUTH

Kursk

XXXX 4 HOTH

Sumy

XXXX 6 PAULUS

Poliava

Desna

XXXX 2 JANY
Glukonov

Konotop

Lubny

Cherkassy

Kiev

Kremenchung

XXXXX B BOCK/WEICHS

Kirovo

Nikolayev

Dnieper

Krivoi Rog

XXXX 1 KLEIST

UKRAINE

N

100 miles
100km

Front line, 7 May 1942
Front line, 23 July 1942
German units
Soviet units
Hungarian units
Romanian units

The Opposing Sides

IDEOLOGY AND RECRUITMENT

Waffen-SS soldier

While ideology of one form or another is sewn through any armed force, as the thread that binds individuals together in unit cohesion, on the Eastern Front the war between Nazism and Communism was almost mythically explicit, and any assessment of the clash between the Waffen-SS and the Red Army's riflemen must explore the motivating factors on each side.

Rapid insight into Waffen-SS ideology comes via the oath that all SS men took upon joining the ranks of Hitler's elite: 'I swear to you, Adolf Hitler, as Führer and Chancellor of the German Reich, my loyalty and bravery. I pledge obedience unto death to you and to your appointed leaders. So help me God.' The implications of this oath are more apparent when we set it against the oath pledged, from March 1935, by the millions of men who entered the wider Wehrmacht:

> I swear to God this holy oath,
> that I shall give my unconditional obedience
> to the Leader of the German Reich and people,
> Adolf Hitler, supreme commander of the armed forces,
> and that as a brave soldier I shall always be ready
> to risk my life for this oath.

In the Wehrmacht oath, the soldier makes the declaration to God as the supreme authority, but devolves spiritual obedience onto the earthly person of Adolf Hitler, particularly in relation to his state leadership functions and his role as the overarching *Oberster Befehlshaber der Wehrmacht* (Supreme Commander of the Armed Forces). This oath brings a commitment to make

the ultimate sacrifice in battle, or at least be 'prepared' to do so. The Waffen-SS, oath, by contrast, places Hitler far more centre stage. The Waffen-SS soldier is there to serve the Führer above all things, temporal and spiritual; God is there merely to 'help' the soldier fulfil his commitment. A crucial sentence is 'I pledge obedience unto death to you and those you appoint to lead'. Strictly taken, the phrasing implies that the soldier's life *will* be given in a state of subjugation to Hitler and, crucially, to senior unit commanders. There is a death-drive at the heart of the Waffen-SS oath, the soldier sacrificing his life on the altar of Nazism.

Who were the men who took this oath, and what was their motivation for doing so? We can start by looking at the baselines established by the beginning of World War II. Crucially, Waffen-SS soldiers were volunteers, not conscripts. They had to have a high degree of physical fitness (Waffen-SS physical training demands were typically higher than those of Heer training), perfect teeth and eyesight, a minimum height of 1.70m for most infantry units and between 17 and 25 years of age for infantry, armoured and signal units (older soldiers could be recruited for other branches of the Waffen-SS). There were variations in these policies within the ranks of the organization. For example, *LSSAH* recruited men of 1.78m minimum height and 25–35 years of age, while in mountain SS units the minimum height could be as low as 1.67m (low-down traction was advantageous in mountainous terrain). Regardless of their physical attributes, every Waffen-SS soldier had to prove he was of 'pure Aryan ancestry' (i.e. with no trace of Jewish blood) back to 1800, a good citizen (no criminal record) and a committed Nazi in ideology. The enlistment period was 25 years for officers, 12 years for NCOs and 4½ years

ABOVE LEFT
In improvised snow camouflage typical of that worn during the winter of 1941–42, a soldier of the SS-Panzergrenadier-Regiment *Der Führer* (SS-Division *Reich*) studies the battlefield with binoculars. His left collar tab insignia indicates that he is an *SS-Unterscharführer*, a junior squad leader. Note the way he has laid two *Stielhandgranaten* across the tops of his rifle magazines. (AirSeaLand/Cody Images)

ABOVE RIGHT
Soldiers of the SS-Totenkopf-Division on the Eastern Front in the summer of 1942. The man at the front is SS-Untersturmführer August Zingel, who was awarded the Knight's Cross of the Iron Cross in 1942. He has MP 40 magazine pouches worn over his camouflage jacket. (AirSeaLand/Cody Images)

This soldier's rank, an NCO rank roughly equivalent to corporal in the Western Allied armies, is denoted by his left collar tab. The *SS-Rottenführer* typically acted as an assistant squad leader, although he might lead a squad in the absence (through casualties or manpower shortages) of an *SS-Unterscharführer* (junior squad leader). Waffen-SS squad leaders were typically armed with SMGs. The soldier is in his early twenties, and a veteran of the Eastern Front having served there since June 1941.

Weapons, dress and equipment

This Waffen-SS *Panzergrenadier* has armed himself with a Soviet 7.62mm PPSh-41 SMG (**1**). The Waffen-SS had no cultural problem with using enemy weapons; indeed, the adoption of foreign-made weapons had been a procurement necessity during the formative years of the Waffen-SS.

Head protection is provided by an M42 helmet with Type II Oak B cover (**2**). His main outer garment is an M42 Type II reversible camouflage smock with Plane Tree camouflage pattern (**3**). This garment was one of a diverse series of camouflage smocks produced for or adopted by the Waffen-SS, and by 1942–43 they had become something of a signature feature of Waffen-SS combat troops. Note the loops sewn onto the shoulder and chest; these were used to affix

camouflaging foliage. Other items of dress include M42 trousers (**4**) tucked into M37 gaiters (**5**), the latter enclosing the tops of the M37 *Schürschuhe* ankle boots (**6**), a more practical alternative to the older calf-length *Marschstiefel* (marching boots).

In terms of equipment, the Waffen-SS tended to go into combat very light, leaving heavy bags and equipment either in vehicles or at a storage location. His Y-straps (**7**) and belt (**8**) support a gas-mask container (**9**), often used to store personal items rather than the gas mask itself, an M42 canteen (**10**), M42 mess kit (**11**) and a bread bag (**12**), which was a useful piece of kit for carrying multiple grenades. The only non-standard piece of kit is the canvas PPSh-41 drum magazine pouch (**13**).

for other ranks. Officers had to have served for two years in the ranks or have an equivalent experience in the Heer.

The motivation to volunteer for the Waffen-SS, at least in the 1930s and the early 1940s, was undoubtedly helped by the organization's public image. Clad in distinctive black uniforms, wrapped in concepts of brotherhood and service, and infused with the Nazi warrior spirit, the Waffen-SS had a certain appeal to young men seeking adventure, status and personal power. The Waffen-SS also had an interesting demographic profile. It proportionately attracted more men from rural backgrounds than the Heer, which generally resulted in higher levels of physical fitness and instinctive field craft but lower levels of education (Quarrie 1993: 18).

By 1942–43, the Waffen-SS had undergone a profound change in its recruitment policy through the swelling admission of non-German soldiers into its ranks, primarily as a way to man units depleted by combat losses and compensate for the greater recruiting power of the Heer. The practice actually began in 1940 when Himmler, with Hitler's blessing, looked to recruit soldiers of Aryan 'related stock' from conquered nations, forming them initially into 'legions' that over time often achieved full divisional status. What began with an influx of Danes, Dutch, Norwegians, Swedes and Finns eventually expanded to include peoples from almost every corner of the expanded Reich and its allies, including Lithuanians, Latvians, Estonians, Hungarians, Italians, Russians, Ukrainians, Serbians, Croatians, even a smattering of British. A formation of particular relevance to this study is the SS-Division *Wiking*, created from early international volunteer units from Denmark, Norway, Sweden, Finland, Estonia, the Netherlands and Belgium.

Although the foreign Waffen-SS units were mostly led by German officers, their dramatic expansion certainly diluted the ideals of the specifically German elite that were part of the Waffen-SS's pre-war and early-war identity. Some of the foreign divisions fought competently and even skilfully, but others did not cover themselves in glory, particularly in the years 1943–45, when more and more Waffen-SS divisions were desperately packaged together in response to the endlessly mounting losses of a falling Reich. There was a psychological division, therefore, between the elite 'old guard' Waffen-SS divisions formed prior to 1943 and those that came later (with some notable exceptions, such as the 12. SS-Panzer-Division *Hitlerjugend*), which included execrable formations such as SS-Obersturmführer Oskar Dirlewanger's 36. Waffen-Grenadier-Division der SS (also known as the Dirlewanger Brigade), with ranks composed of murderers, rapists and other criminals – such units were poles apart from the original standards set for the Waffen-SS. A key point to bear in mind, however, is that the Waffen-SS units and formations studied in this book were still of the elite mindset, and were exclusively loyal to their divisional and regimental identity, seeing the unit as the ultimate horizon for their lives and deaths.

Soviet rifleman

When we turn our attention to the Soviet rifleman, we step into a very different world. Although there were certainly many Red Army volunteers, particularly in the first months of the Great Patriotic War (1941–45), most

of the *frontoviki* ('front fighters') were drawn into the ranks via conscription. By 1942, the conscription age for Soviet soldiers was 18 for those without a secondary education and 19 for those with such an education. The latter were in the minority, however; the literacy and numeracy levels of Soviet riflemen were often pitifully low, especially as men with higher levels of education were often creamed off for political service in the Naródnyy Komissariát Vnútrennikh Del (NKVD; People's Commissariat of Internal Affairs).

Soviet soldiers came from all walks of life, but the front-line infantryman predominantly hailed from the urban or rural working class, individuals often familiar with poverty and hardship, which goes a long way to explaining their tremendous fortitude in military service. As with the Waffen-SS, social origins could make a practical difference in combat; again, soldiers with rural upbringings had inbuilt advantages in terms of life on campaign – in creating convincing camouflage, for example. In peacetime, the terms of military service for private soldiers were two years on active duty, three years on furlough (during which period he could be recalled immediately) and reserve status until 50 years old. In wartime, the concept of terms of service largely collapsed: the soldier would serve until he was either wounded, killed, released for special reasons or the war ended.

As a window into the ideology and motivations of the Soviet rifleman, the oath of the Soviet soldier stands in useful contrast to that of the Waffen-SS soldier:

> I_____, a citizen of the Union of the Soviet Socialist Republics, entering into the ranks of the Red Army of the Workers and Peasants, take this oath and solemnly promise to be an honest, brave, disciplined, vigilant fighter, staunchly to protect military and state secrets, and unquestioningly to obey all military regulations and orders of commanders and superiors.

Two Red Army riflemen fight for the ruins of a hamlet in the Voronezh sector in 1942. Both are armed with the SVT-40 semi-automatic rifle. It was initially intended that about one-third of Red Army rifle-division soldiers would be armed with SVTs, but by 1942 the production focus had shifted forward to SMGs and backward to Mosin-Nagant M1891/30 bolt-action rifles. (AirSeaLand/Cody Images)

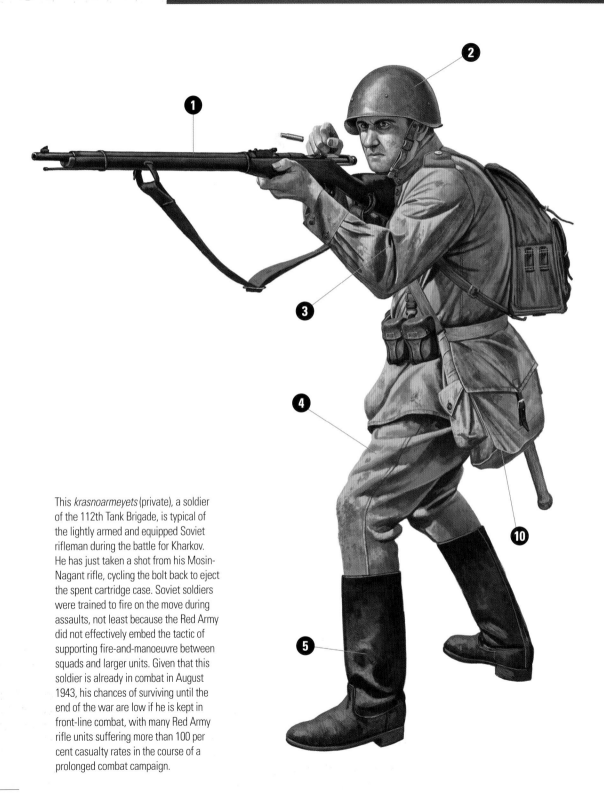

This *krasnoarmeyets* (private), a soldier of the 112th Tank Brigade, is typical of the lightly armed and equipped Soviet rifleman during the battle for Kharkov. He has just taken a shot from his Mosin-Nagant rifle, cycling the bolt back to eject the spent cartridge case. Soviet soldiers were trained to fire on the move during assaults, not least because the Red Army did not effectively embed the tactic of supporting fire-and-manoeuvre between squads and larger units. Given that this soldier is already in combat in August 1943, his chances of surviving until the end of the war are low if he is kept in front-line combat, with many Red Army rifle units suffering more than 100 per cent casualty rates in the course of a prolonged combat campaign.

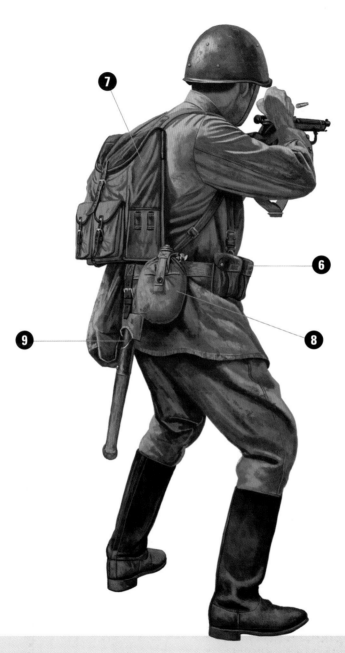

Weapons, dress and equipment

The 7.62mm Mosin-Nagant M1891/30 rifle (**1**) was the standard-issue Soviet rifle of World War II. Although it was intended to be operated as standard with its long spike bayonet, this item was often omitted by soldiers in combat, particularly those fighting in urban or close-quarters terrain.

His head protection is the SSh-40 steel helmet (**2**), identified by the lower position of the shell rivets compared with the earlier SSh-39. He wears the M43 summer tunic (**3**), which displays simple shoulder straps with the raspberry piping to denote infantry (infantry uniforms had no unit identification), matched with the M41 summer breeches (**4**) tucked into black leather marching boots (**5**).

Ammunition stripper clips for his rifle are held in the four leather pouches (**6**) on the enlisted man's belt. Other items of kit are the M39 canvas backpack (**7**), a water flask (**8**) and entrenching tool (**9**), plus the SM-1 gas-mask bag (**10**), which like the German practice was often used to carry grenades.

I promise conscientiously to study military affairs, in every way to protect state secrets and state property, and to my last breath to be faithful to the people, the Soviet Motherland, and the Workers-Peasants' Government. I am always prepared on order of the Workers and Peasants Government to rise to the defence of my Motherland, the Union of Soviet Socialist Republics; and as a fighting man of the Red Army of Workers and Peasants, I promise to defend it bravely, skilfully, with dignity and honour, sparing neither my blood nor my life itself for the achievement of total victory over our enemies.

If by evil intent I should violate this, my solemn oath, then let the severe punishment of Soviet law and the total hatred and contempt of the working classes befall me. (Rottman 2007: 11–12)

Obviously, this oath is considerably longer than that of the Waffen-SS, and it is interesting to explore the differences. Like the German oath, the Soviet version is ideologically aligned, although it disconnects the communist ideology from a single authoritarian figurehead – the Soviet soldier is loyal to the nation, state government and, implicitly, the overarching principles of socialism. The last paragraph truly hammers home the moral and judicial consequences of disobedience; in the absence of references to God (another key distinction from German oaths), failure to obey the socialist vision results in an atheistic equivalent of being damned to hell.

There is a clear focus on unquestioning obedience to superiors, and this is not mere authoritarianism. The Red Army was an entity seemingly without horizons. By war's end, an estimated 34 million men had passed through Soviet wartime military service. About 75 per cent of the Red Army consisted of rifle (infantry) divisions. Governing this mass of manpower would be difficult enough in peacetime, but under wartime conditions it became an exercise in chaos management, not least because of the scale of the losses – 4 million Soviet casualties in the first six months of fighting – and the deep German occupation of western Soviet territories.

The Soviet rifleman's oath had to embrace and govern a wide range of ethnic diversity. At this time, the Soviet Union contained more than 100 ethnic groups, albeit weighted heavily (85 per cent) towards the Slavic peoples of Russia, Ukraine and Byelorussia (modern-day Belarus). In most cases, multiple ethnicities were incorporated into individual units in a process of *sliianie* ('blending'), with some non-ethnic exceptions (such as Cossack units). *Sliianie* ensured that potential nationalistic alignments were fragmented and controlled in the armed forces, but it also meant that unit commanders had to handle units with mixed languages (although Russian was the official military language) and diverse social and cultural backgrounds, compounded by the poor levels of education noted above. Partly for this reason, and partly from the state's political paranoia, the Soviet rifleman was built to be a creature of unswerving obedience, as the oath reflects.

In the Waffen-SS, political ideals were often born from enthusiastic political conversion to National Socialism, encouraged by Joseph Goebbels' propaganda machine. In the Red Army, by contrast, ideological commitment to the ideals of Soviet communism was generally ingrained through long-standing and far-reaching indoctrination from infancy through adulthood. Until roughly half-way through our period of study in this book, political

komissars (commissars) – aided by legions of embedded *seksot'* ('secret collaborators', i.e. informers) – kept invasive watch over the political reliability of both commanders and men, the commissars embedded in the command structure down to battalion level, and having equal authority with the unit commanders. In 1941–42 the commissars progressively lost their authority over tactical decision-making and were made subordinate to military commanding officers, as it was finally recognized that political interference could often compromise military effectiveness. Thus the commissar was redesignated as *politruk* (deputy commander for political affairs), although officers and men still had to maintain deep compliance with the Communist Party line.

Ultimately, the Soviet rifleman was likely more motivated to fight, and fight very hard, by the simple fact that the war on the Eastern Front was an existential one: Hitler's forces intended to destroy the Soviet state and, at a literal level, enslave or exterminate its people, whom it classified as *Untermenschen* (subhumans, inferior people). The fire-hardened Nazism of the Waffen-SS was the embodiment of this outlook. In the ranks of the Soviet riflemen, by contrast, there were doubtless many committed communists, but it is often difficult to separate them out from the mass of soldiers whose lives were simply soaked through with the compliance of living in a communist dictatorship. What united them all, however, was a general contempt for the *fashistkii* (fascists), who through their oath they committed to drive from their lands.

ABOVE LEFT
Every Red Army rifle regiment had two reconnaissance platoons (one mounted, one on foot). The men within them were trained to higher standards in field craft and small-unit combat, and often had a leading role in helping to decide lines of attack. The man at the front is armed with a PPD-40 SMG, which was replaced by the more economical PPSh-41 in 1941. (AirSeaLand/Cody Images)

ABOVE RIGHT
This Soviet rifleman is wearing heavy winter clothing, including the thick felt overboots, the *vatnie sharovari* padded trousers and the *telogreika* padded jacket, topped by the defining *shapka-ushanka* fur hat. Note the way he uses his left hand to form a stable shooting base for his PPSh-41. (AirSeaLand/Cody Images)

19

TRAINING AND TACTICS

Waffen-SS soldier

Looking through the prism of training gives a deeper understanding of the fundamental differences in battlefield performance between the Waffen-SS soldier and the Red Army rifleman. The Waffen-SS prided itself on inculcating very high levels of physical fitness and tactical initiative. The length of training varied considerably during the war years, especially during the second half of the conflict, and also had contrasts between the divisions, but typically it lasted about 4–6 months. Physical fitness and mental courage were merged into one training package. The Waffen-SS recruit underwent bruising unarmed-combat instruction in which blows were landed with intent and ferocity, including with weapons such as rifle stocks and sheathed bayonets. Boxing, wrestling and ju-jitsu were standard elements of the training curriculum, as were frequent assault courses and route marches in full kit. Small-unit 'battles' were regularly conducted, both testing and developing tactical initiative down to individual soldier level. There was a particularly high premium placed on weapon handling, with the soldiers spending many hours sending rounds down-range and in exercises that enhanced both their marksmanship and tactical intelligence, such as understanding the optimal configurations of machine-gun and mortar support fire for an infantry assault.

Most distinctively, the Waffen-SS prided itself on the heavy use of live ammunition during tactical exercises. This practice was somewhat controversial, as the inevitable accidents produced a constant trickle of injuries and fatalities. In the Waffen-SS mindset, however, the risk was worth the reward. The brutality of the training bred hard men (or unmasked those

Waffen-SS grenadiers ride on an assortment of PzKpfw III and IV medium tanks as they prepare to counter-attack in Ukraine during 1943. The tanks would help the infantry by engaging enemy armour and providing long-range direct fire support against enemy strongpoints; the infantry would protect the armour from enemy infantry anti-tank teams and had better visual awareness of the terrain. (AirSeaLand/Cody Images)

A Waffen-SS 7.5cm PaK 40 anti-tank gun crew make ready to engage a target. The low profile of the gun, as evident here, and its excellent penetration capabilities (120mm at 500m on armour at 30 degrees from the vertical) made it a high-kill weapon system in good hands – see the number of 'kill' rings on the barrel. (AirSeaLand/Cody Images)

who weren't), used to physical pain and the sound of bullets cracking past their heads even before they reached the battlefield. Other forms of what we would today refer to as 'battle inoculation' included nerve-jangling exercises such as having the men dig foxholes in which they then crouched as tanks drove over the top of them. (Such exercises would actually have practical relevance on the Eastern Front.) They also, unlike the soldiers of the Heer, received formal lectures each week in National Socialist theory, with particular emphasis on racial and political doctrines, fusing physical toughness with ideological fervour.

In terms of tactical training, the Waffen-SS focused on combined-arms cooperation, especially between infantry, armour, artillery and support aircraft, and small-unit initiative, the latter producing exceptionally high standards among NCOs and junior combat leaders. Tactical coherence was helped by unit loyalty, which was critically important in the Waffen-SS. Unlike the Heer, which might often form improvised *Kampfgruppen* (battlegroups) by combining units from different divisions, the Waffen-SS tended to keep its formations unified, even to the point of their destruction, to maintain the internal *esprit de corps* for which the Waffen-SS became renowned. Tactical training and exercises, from squad to divisional levels, emphasized a mission-oriented attitude, in which it was acceptable for front-line troops to adapt plans freely 'on the fly' to achieve mission success. The doctrine of decentralized tactical initiative was, of course, not purely a Waffen-SS property, but was also advocated in the Wehrmacht at large. A US intelligence observer stated that:

> The prime characteristic of German tactical doctrine is maintenance of the initiative and avoidance of stabilization. The Germans believe absolutely that if a trained commander prepares and executes aggressive moves, with even average ability and reasonable speed, the enemy will be kept too busy meeting them to carry out successful offensive measures. (Military Intelligence Service 1942: 29)

The German armed forces certainly emphasized in training, and lauded in public, examples of audacious action taken by often-photogenic commanders.

Waffen-SS troops engage in street fighting in Kharkov in 1943. The soldier second from the left is an assistant gunner, indicated by his carrying a box of 7.92×57mm ammunition plus a spare barrel in the long metal container. (AirSeaLand/Cody Images)

By 1942, one much-publicized example of tactical dash was that of SS-Hauptsturmführer Fritz Klingenberg, a company commander in the *Kradschützen-Bataillon* (motorcycle rifle battalion) of the SS-Division *Reich* (from May 1942, known as *Das Reich*). With just six men under his leadership during operations in Yugoslavia in April 1941, and wilfully modifying higher orders, Klingenberg managed to surpass the efforts of the entire 11. Panzer-Division and essentially force the surrender of the Belgrade garrison, bluffing the local mayor into thinking that he would summon an air strike on the city if it did not lay down its arms, even though Klingenberg had no means of communication with the Luftwaffe. For this action he was awarded the *Ritterkreuz* (Knight's Cross). Klingenberg, and a growing pantheon of Waffen-SS heroes and leaders, embodied what Wehrmacht military doctrine outlined as tactical innovation, here translated in the wartime US Military Intelligence Service manual *The German Squad in Combat*:

> In the execution of battle missions, one should be most careful to avoid the idea that only one solution can be the right one. Only success in an actual case could prove that a given solution was the right one. A model solution must not be drilled into the soldiers. They, and particularly the squad leader, should be trained to be flexible, and should learn to be equal to any occasion. (Quoted in Military Intelligence Service 1943: 30)

The Waffen-SS was perfectly structured to deliver tactical initiative, as it had an adaptable attitude to unit composition and weapons distribution, trained men to think independently, invested in tactical knowledge and also fostered a mindset comfortable with elevated levels of risk and reward.

Soviet rifleman

The training experience of the great majority of Soviet riflemen during wartime was truly worlds apart from that of the Waffen-SS, particularly in 1941–43. In peacetime, training typically lasted about 6–12 months, but during the war years the need to push men rapidly into the front lines reduced instruction programmes to a few cursory and inadequate weeks. Furthermore, the training within this time frame was often amateurish and unfocused.

Several issues combined to affect the quality of rifleman training. The first was logistical. The austerity of a war economy meant that basic items of personal equipment and training facilities were often lacking. This situation was particularly acute in relation to weapons training. Many recruits might go to their front-line unit having fired fewer than ten rounds from a rifle, without any requirement to demonstrate competent marksmanship. Lack of available weapons and ammunition might mean that the soldier was not even issued a rifle or SMG until he reached the front-line unit, and then he would take it into action without having zeroed the sights on a range (Rottman 2007: 14). Experience in weapon handling, therefore, was gained primarily through combat experience, the steepest of all learning curves. The Waffen-SS's focus on making weapon handling utterly fluid and automatic through constant live firing and practice was not a possibility for the Soviet forces during these years.

The second major issue was a lack of functional tactical training. Unlike the Waffen-SS, the Red Army did not encourage anything approaching individual initiative, and largely focused on instilling unquestioning obedience to orders. There was often little opportunity or will to conduct realistic and repeated field exercises, thus men headed into battle with little more than a theoretical

Soviet riflemen, like infantrymen on all sides, often rode into battle on tanks and dismounted for combat. These soldiers, pictured in 1942, are to a man armed with PPSh-41 SMGs, apart from the individual with his left hand on the tank's gun barrel, who appears to have a German MP 40. (AirSeaLand/ Cody Images)

knowledge delivered through readings of the official Red Army manuals of the day, the soldiers standing or sitting in serried ranks and listening passively to tactical doctrine, read aloud by their commanders. (Soldiers would often be kept standing to attention during these lectures to prevent them from dozing off.) The problems of delivering practical combat training were compounded by the fact that there was often a severe shortage of experienced and qualified instructors, due to combat losses and also because those who possessed such knowledge were in-demand at the front.

Red Army training did undergo something of a progressive evolution during the war years, however, beginning during the time frame of this book. (More about the evolution of Waffen-SS and Soviet infantry tactics will be discussed in the 'Analysis' section below.) Up until the autumn of 1942, the main handbook of Red Army infantry doctrine and tactics was the 1938 edition of the *Handbook for Infantrymen of the Workers and Peasants Red Army of the Union of Soviet Socialist Republics*. In November 1942 a new edition of the manual was produced, which conceptually incorporated both the harrowing lessons of disaster from 1941 plus the recognition that the Red Army needed to become a more intelligent, flexible entity if it was to win the war. Note, for example, how the manual now portrayed the infantry as one element in combined-arms operations, and recognized that coordination between the branches needed to be rooted psychologically in the manpower:

> 5. The present Manual regards operations conducted by the Infantry as those of combined arms and services with a wide participation of various combat technique: all types of artillery, tanks, and aircraft. They require precision and well organized coordination of all arms and services.
>
> Commanding personnel of the Infantry must always bear in mind the absolute necessity of uninterrupted coordination during combat of all units participating in it. It is being urged to master the new organization methods outlined in the Manual. (Department of Defense 1951: 4)

The manual does not go so far as to free the rifleman from undeviating compliance with orders, but it does imply that professionalism and skill, especially in the combined-arms context, were going to be central for future victories. Historian Catherine Merridale notes (2006: 320–22) that in the autumn of 1942 the Red Army high command began to issue more detailed demands for improved tactical training, particularly attempting to improve the poor coordination and liaison between infantry, artillery and armour. This prompted an increased emphasis on practical combat drills during training, including participation in some combined-arms exercises. These improvements started to filter through to the battlefield in earnest during 1943–44, as evidenced by the Red Army's noticeable offensive confidence.

Regardless of the improvements, however, it was still the case in general that the Red Army rifleman's training fell well below the standards of that of the Waffen-SS, or at least the Waffen-SS divisions formed before the precipitous collapse of the Third Reich in 1944–45. Much of the rifleman's tactical skill, therefore, would be acquired directly through the experience of operations. This was not necessarily a bad route to understanding, as long as the soldier could survive enough initial encounters to learn key lessons.

Front-line NCOs and junior officers were also critically important in providing practical knowledge, and small-unit relationships and loyalties were often especially strong, not least because Soviet riflemen had the additional motivation of unleashing vengeance on the enemy that had ruined much of their country. One of the key differences between the Waffen-SS soldier and the Soviet rifleman was that while the former fought for ideology, the latter fought for genuine survival – one of the most powerful motivators of all.

WEAPONS

Waffen-SS soldier

At the infantry level, both the Waffen-SS and the Red Army rifle divisions were still substantially equipped with bolt-action, magazine-fed rifles. For the Waffen-SS, this meant the standard-issue Kar 98k rifle, chambered for the 7.92×57mm Mauser cartridge. Based on photographic evidence, limited numbers of Waffen-SS troops were issued with Germany's first forays into semi-automatic rifles, the 7.92mm Gew 41 and the subsequent Gew 43 (in the same calibre), which served as assault-type weapons and as sniping rifles when fitted with telescopic sights. Although both types offered the undoubted advantages of semi-automatic fire – greater volumes of fire, large magazine capacities, the ability to switch between targets without taking one's head off the stock and one's eyes off the sights, fast magazine changes – both weapons had significant reliability issues; and production volumes were limited and stretched between the Heer and the Waffen-SS. (The Waffen-SS did acquire significant numbers (although from only 426,000 produced) of the highly effective 7.92mm MP 43/MP 44/StG 44 *Sturmgewehr*, the weapon that truly established the assault-rifle type, but these acquisitions appeared after the time period studied here.)

Close-quarters fighting was the province of submachine guns (SMGs) and pistols. By the early years of the war, the Waffen-SS had acquired a more diverse range of SMG types than the Heer, including the 9mm Erma EMP, Bergmann MP 28, Steyr MP 34 and Bergmann MP 35, as well as the new MP 38 designed by Heinrich Vollmer. Some Erma, Steyr and Bergmann SMGs persisted in Waffen-SS hands into the 1942–43 period, not least because they were of high-quality build and because their horizontal magazine arrangement was preferred by some to the MP 38/40, but they were used in very small numbers and generally found in the hands of SS police and security units. As in the Heer, therefore, the Waffen-SS used the standard German 9mm MP 38 and MP 40 SMGs, the latter being the more cost-effective variant and therefore the more common by 1942–43. The MP 38/40 were sound firearms. The type's c.550rd/min rate of fire was steady and controllable with little recoil and muzzle climb, making for a reasonably accurate weapon over 100–200m effective ranges, and one that could also be fired comfortably from the hip during close assaults. The one flaw was its magazine – its long vertical arrangement made the MP 38/40 awkward for prone shooting and the double-stack to single-feed ammunition arrangement was prone to misfeeds. The Waffen-SS frequently acquired and made use of Soviet PPSh-41 SMGs, appreciated because of its robust battlefield performance and astonishing close-quarters firepower.

Pistols were largely, but not exclusively, the province of Waffen-SS officers, who leaned towards compact types such as the Walther PP and PPK (which came in a variety of calibres) or the standard-issue 9mm Luger P 08 and the Walther P 38. Although the former is more famous, the latter is actually a superior weapon in terms of functionality and safety and was particularly preferred by the Waffen-SS; the head of the SS procurement office, SS-Brigadeführer Heinrich Gärtner, even tried to secure *all* P 38 production for the SS, something he failed to achieve (Quarrie 1993: 12). Another popular handgun in use with the Waffen-SS was the Belgian 9mm Browning Hi-Power, a pre-war design that carried 13 rounds in its magazine; by comparison, the P 38 carried just eight.

Exhaustion lies heavy upon these Waffen-SS soldiers. The soldier in the foreground is methodically cleaning his Kar 98k rifle; a build-up of dust or dirt in the bolt mechanism could result in a failure to feed or extract a cartridge. Adopted in June 1935, the Kar 98k had a five-round internal magazine, loaded via a stripper clip pressed down into the magazine. The rifle had an effective range of about 500m with the iron sights, but more than double that range when equipped with a telescopic sight. (Some Waffen-SS squads would include at least one rifleman-sniper, for precision long-range fire.) The Kar 98k can appear as a poor relative of more sophisticated Waffen-SS small arms, but it still represented the pinnacle of bolt-action rifle design, and was a reasonably effective weapon in well-trained hands: c.15 aimed shots per minute was possible for someone with a well-honed firing and reloading technique. Its main deficiencies from a handling point of view were its low magazine capacity, the way the bolt handle obscured the sights when it was in its upright position (interfering with fast follow-up shots), thumping recoil (again, not helping with accurate follow-up shots) and a less-than-satisfactory safety switch on the rear of the bolt. (AirSeaLand/Cody Images)

An SdKfz 232 eight-wheel heavy command vehicle of the SS-Panzergrenadier-Division *Wiking* on the Eastern Front, a crew member sitting on the distinctive high-mounted frame aerial. The vehicle was fitted with a 2cm cannon and an MG 34 general-purpose machine gun for anti-personnel defence. (AirSeaLand/Cody Images)

Pistols were not just carried by officers. They made their way into the hands of the rank-and-file as well, if only as battlefield booty and exceptional acquisitions, but they were also usefully carried as back-up weapons by support-fire teams and auxiliary troops. One weapon of particular note in this regard was the Mauser C96 'Broomhandle' pistol, for use with 7.63×25mm or 9×19mm cartridges. By 1942, however, the C96 was practically an antique (it was in service from 1896) and an oddity in terms of its layout, with an integral box magazine located in front of the trigger, a top-heavy weight distribution and a broom-like grip. It also had a wooden holster that could double as a shoulder stock, and in this configuration it was a useful instrument for close-quarters fighting, particularly in the powerful 7.63×25mm calibre. There is photographic evidence of Waffen-SS soldiers engaging targets with this weapon set-up during 1942–43.

While the Waffen-SS were keen adopters of good foreign weapons, when it came to heavier support fire they rarely took others' firearms, preferring instead the superb 7.92mm MG 34 and MG 42, two of the finest 'general-purpose machine guns' ever made. The weapons could be fired from their integral bipods but also from a variety of other mounts – tripods (for sustained and indirect fire), pintle mounts, anti-aircraft mounts, tank ball mounts – each mount changing the weapon's tactical utility. A rapid barrel-change facility enabled the Waffen-SS gunner and assistant gunner to swap out an overheating barrel for a cool one in just seconds. With its rate of fire of *c.*1,200rd/min, the MG 42's contribution to weight of support fire was undeniable, as we shall see in the Third Battle of Kharkov in February–March 1943.

One of the other essential tools of infantry combat was the hand grenade. The most common hand grenade of the Waffen-SS, like the Heer, was the M24 *Stielhandgranate* (stick hand grenade), and its simplified successor, the M43. The wooden handle on the M24 not only gave extra leverage behind the throw; it was also useful for sticking into belts to keep the grenades at instant readiness. Waffen-SS soldiers can also be seen in photographs with their bread bags filled with grenades during urban combat as they were extremely useful for room clearance (effective lethal radius was about 15m). In addition to the stick grenades, however, the Waffen-SS also carried several other types, including the M39 *Eihandgranate* (egg hand grenade) and a selection of anti-armour and demolition types for stronger blast effects.

Soviet rifleman

The defining weapon of the Russian rifleman was the 7.62mm Mosin-Nagant M1891/30 rifle. Offering similar performance characteristics to the Kar 98k, the M1891/30 was a bolt-action rifle with a five-round integral box magazine (loaded with either individual rounds or stripper clips); it had an effective range of about 500m with iron sights but substantially more when fitted with a scope; it was reliable and had similar rates of fire in trained hands. It was, however, nearly 12.5cm longer than the Kar 98k, which made it less convenient to handle in close-quarters combat.

The Red Army was one of the first armies to adopt semi-automatic rifles on a significant scale, although without the technical and tactical success of the US Army's move to the M1 Garand. The types available during our period of study were three 7.62mm weapons: the Simonov AVS-36, the Tokarev SVT-38 and the Tokarev SVT-40. All three offered the same on-paper tactical advantages of semi-auto firearms outlined above. They were gas-operated, the AVS-36 feeding from a 15-round detachable box magazine (this also had a selective-fire feature, so it could be fired as an LMG from a bipod), the SVT-38 and -40 from a ten-round equivalent. But mechanical problems and design flaws dogged the weapons. The AVS-36 had challenging muzzle blast and recoil, and an unreliable locking mechanism, and only 65,800 were manufactured. Its 1939 replacement, the SVT-38, was a better prospect in design, but it remained unreliable under the harsh conditions of the Eastern Front, so the improved and strengthened variant, the SVT-

This image of a machine-gun team and squad commander from the SS-Panzergrenadier-Division *Leibstandarte SS Adolf Hitler* (*LSSAH*) shows the MG 42 GPMG's long barrel-change slot down the right-hand side of the barrel jacket. The assistant gunner carries a spare ammunition belt; other members of the squad would often also do the same. (AirSeaLand/Cody Images)

40, was its replacement from April 1940. More than 1 million of these rifles were produced in 1941, but poor production standards meant that many were prone to stoppages and breakages. They were also far more complex for the average Red Army rifleman to use (many of the rifles were fitted with telescopic sights and used as sniping rifles), thus production of the SVT-40 dropped low after 1941, in favour of the basic Mosin-Nagant rifle.

When it came to Soviet infantry combat in 1942–43, however, the game-changing weapon was the 7.62mm PPSh-41. This ultra-robust SMG could deliver fire a rate of somewhere between 900 and 1,200rd/min, feeding from either a 35-round box magazine or – better still, considering the rate of fire – a 71-round drum magazine. This firepower was a blistering compensation for the Red Army's generally poor standards of marksmanship training; SMG-

armed riflemen could fire rapid multi-round bursts that to some degree compensated for inaccuracy, not least because the soldier could 'walk' visible impacts onto his target. The Red Army also tended to use crude skirmish-line tactics during the assault, not the fire-and-manoeuvre leapfrogging of units practised by the German forces. Fired on the move, the PPSh-41 could therefore provide, to a degree and over a range of up to 250m, a measure of suppressive fire. For these reasons, production of the PPSh-41 and the distribution of SMGs was massively ramped up in the Red Army from the late summer of 1941. In 1942 alone, about 1.5 million PPSh-41s were produced, thus the Waffen-SS fighting in 1942 and 1943 would have been very familiar with being on the receiving end of these weapons, and were so convinced by its merits that they often took and used them as their own.

The work of heavier automatic fire suppression was delivered by a collection of light, medium and heavy machine guns, principally: the Maxim-type weapons, especially the 7.62mm PM M1910 and PM M1910/30; the Degtyaryov family of machine guns, specifically the 7.62mm DP and DPM light machine guns (LMGs), the 7.62mm DS-39 medium machine gun (MMG) and the 12.7mm DShK and DShKM heavy machine guns (HMGs); and the 7.62mm Goryunov SG-43 MMG. The most common types in use during the 1942–43 period were: at squad level, the DP LMG, a fixed-barrel gas-operated weapon firing at 550rd/min from a 47-round pan magazine; the PM M1910/30 – basically a heavy water-cooled Maxim gun fired from a wheeled cart – in the hands of company-level machine-gun squads; and the bruising DShK, essentially an anti-aircraft weapon, but on a wheeled mount it could be re-purposed to deliver pulverizing ground fire.

The Soviet forces lacked a weapon that fulfilled the GPMG concept fulfilled by the Germans' MG 34 and MG 42. The DP had the mobility, but its fixed barrel and magazine feed limited the firepower, while the PM M1910/30 had the firepower but lacked the mobility. It is arguably only in the realms of close-quarters fighting that the Soviets enjoyed a firepower advantage, which is why in the street battles of Rostov-on-Don and Kharkov they often stuck so closely to their enemy.

Rostov-on-Don

20–25 July 1942

BACKGROUND TO BATTLE

By the beginning of 1942, it was evident to the Axis Powers that the war was not going in the inexorably victorious direction that Hitler wanted. The years 1939–41 had been all about German triumphs, albeit at severe cost, and the German-occupied territories now stretched from the Atlantic Ocean to the gates of Moscow, and from the Arctic Ocean to the coast of North Africa. As the war approached its third year, however, it was undeniable that the momentum was bleeding out of the Wehrmacht juggernaut, overstretched across multiple fronts, and facing enemies more confident on the offensive.

On the Eastern Front, the brakes had slammed on the German advance thanks to Hitler's mercurial strategic planning, the Russian winter and a resurgent Red Army, reinforcements for which from the East enabled it to launch powerful counter-offensives against Heeresgruppe Mitte (Army Group Centre) in December 1941. In early 1942, Stalin was discovering a bullish new military attitude, expressed particularly in the southern sectors of the Eastern Front through a series of ill-planned and executed offensives against Heeresgruppe Süd (Army Group South). An assault by five armies of the South-West Front and South Front from 18 January between Kharkov (modern-day Kharkiv, Ukraine) and Artemovsk (modern-day Bakhmut, Ukraine) punched a 100km salient into German lines, but by 31 January had run out of force against German defensive lines and 'hedgehog' positions – the Wehrmacht was proving as adept in defence as it was in offence. Spring rains kept the front lines comparatively inactive before, on 12 May, the Soviet forces in the south attempted another heavy push. By this time, however, the German forces on the Eastern Front had received galvanizing influxes of fresh manpower (51 Axis divisions arrived on the Eastern Front in April 1942) and

Red Army anti-tank guns open up on targets on the Eastern Front. Every Red Army rifle division had an artillery regiment (12 122mm, 20 76mm guns) and an anti-tank battalion (12 45mm guns); the 45mm guns were initially the M37 then the longer-barrelled M42, which largely replaced the M37 in 1942. (AirSeaLand/Cody Images)

new *matériel* (particularly superior armour types), and they were ready. The 6. Armee and Panzergruppe Kleist (17. Armee and 1. Panzerarmee) not only reversed the Soviet gains, but also pushed the attackers back beyond their start lines, reaching the entrance to the Donets Basin by the end of May and taking some 240,000 Soviet prisoners in the process. In a month of Axis victories, the 11. Armee also cleared the Kerch Peninsula.

It was now time for Hitler's next big strategic move, codenamed *Fall Blau* (see page 8). In July 1942, one of the major urban objectives of Heeresgruppe A as part of this operation was the city of Rostov-on-Don, a gateway to the western Caucasus and a major road, rail and river traffic hub in the region. By 20 July, two major pincers were closing around the city: the 17. Armee from the west and north-west and the 1. Panzerarmee from the east and the north-east. Operating with the latter was the SS-Division *Wiking*.

Wiking was the first of the major foreign divisions formed within the Waffen-SS, established in December 1940 from Dutch, Danish and Norwegian volunteers around the experienced German cadre of the *Germania* Regiment from the SS-Division *Reich*. It also incorporated Finnish volunteers in 1941. *Fall Blau* would give *Wiking* its first taste of battle, but it was actually going into action around Rostov-on-Don incomplete: it consisted of the SS-Regiment *Germania* and two battalions of the SS-Regiment *Nordland*, all of which were motorized, but its SS-Regiment *Westland* and III./SS-Rgt *Nordland* would not join them until the end of July, by which time Rostov-on-Don had fallen. In balance, *Wiking* had received a new three-company armoured battalion, two companies equipped with PzKpfw III medium tanks and one company of PzKpfw IV medium tanks (each company had 16 tanks in total).

While the armoured Waffen-SS battle in and around Rostov-on-Don is a story unto itself, here we will focus mainly on the infantry actions of one particular motorized detachment, led by the commander of the I./SS-Rgt *Germania*, SS-Sturmbannführer August Hinrich Dieckmann, a highly

decorated officer who had been in action since the beginning of the war. He led a *Kampfgruppe* (battle group) into action at Rostov-on-Don; as well as his battalion of *Panzergrenadiere*, Dieckmann had support from a company of Panzers, three batteries of 10.5cm guns and one battery of 15cm guns, a company of combat engineers, an anti-aircraft platoon equipped with 2cm cannon and a supply column (Tigre 2006/Marini 1980).

The Soviet situation in and around Rostov-on-Don in July 1942 was chaotic. The Red Army's Southern Front, under the command of Lieutenant-General Rodion Yakovlevich Malinovsky, had been falling back from positions north of Rostov-on-Don, unable to stop the German advance but successfully escaping encirclement at Millerovo. Having mostly escaped the trap, the troops of the 12th, 18th and 56th armies retreated progressively towards Rostov-on-Don, Malinovsky having ordered, on 16 July, all forces of the Southern Front to withdraw below the Don River south of Rostov-on-Don (Glantz 2009: 202).

By 20 July, the general demeanour of the Red Army forces in Rostov-on-Don did not signal an intended fight to the death, as occurred later at Stalingrad. Rostov-on-Don had been fortified to resist a German attack and a core of protection was provided by the 70th and 158th Fortified Regions units (special units created to defend a fortified position) and NKVD forces. Much of the Southern Front retreat pushed into and through Rostov-on-Don, but the 18th and, primarily, the 56th Rifle divisions placed forces around the city's defences in an effort to break the German momentum. To the west were the 2nd Guards Rifle Division and the 68th, 76th and 81st Naval Rifle brigades, while to the north and east were the 30th, 339th and 31st Rifle divisions and the 16th Rifle Brigade. The total number of defenders manning the city's outer defences likely numbered around 15,000 men.

Soviet soldiers dig either a large defensive position or the beginnings of an anti-tank ditch, although the job of digging the latter was often performed by civilians from nearby settlements or by special pioneer and fortification units. (AirSeaLand/Cody Images)

MAP KEY

1 20 July: Approximately 15,000 Red Army troops occupy defensive positions protecting the eastern and north-eastern approaches to Rostov-on-Don.

2 20–21 July: With the XXXXIX. Gebirgs-Armeekorps on its right and the 13. Panzer-Division on its left, elements of the SS-Division *Wiking* advance on Rostov-on-Don from the west, diverting north to establish an overnight position just west of Stoiakov.

3 c.0400–2200hrs, 22 July: *Wiking* Panzers and Dieckmann's grenadiers make an assault on the Soviet outer defensive perimeters around Sultan-Saly. Despite heavy resistance and many obstacles, the Waffen-SS forces manage to breach the defences in the late-afternoon hours, clearing the Red Army positions and establishing an eastern bridgehead by 2200hrs.

4 c.0400–1400hrs, 23 July: Waffen-SS troops assault towards heavily defended positions around Leninavan. The progress is at first slow, but Dieckmann makes a flanking manoeuvre with armour and two companies of grenadiers,

securing a bridge crossing further south. The opposition at Leninavan is overcome in the subsequent attack by *Wiking* and the second lines of defences is penetrated.

5 1400–2000hrs, 23 July: The Waffen-SS units drive into Rostov-on-Don, pushing into the city from the east with armour and grenadiers, aided by heavy support fire. Facing intensive street battles, the German troops nevertheless cut through the resistance and establish all-round defensive strongpoints in the southern part of the city, overlooking the Don River.

6 23–25 July: As the Waffen-SS and Heer forces spread out through Rostov-on-Don, many Red Army soldiers evacuate across the Don River. Others, however, alongside NKVD troops, fight on in isolated pockets of resistance until they are finally destroyed. On the German side, the brunt of the street clearance is handled by the Heer's 125. Infanterie-Division, and the Waffen-SS casualties are relatively light during this final phase of the city battle. Personnel of the SS-Division *Wiking* use the occupation of Rostov-on-Don to rest and regroup in preparation for further pushes into the Caucasus.

Battlefield environment

Rostov-on-Don was a critical road and rail hub connecting the Caucasus and southern Russia, and a major port on the Don River, which ran through the south of the city and flowed out into the Sea of Azov some 32km to the west. The city's strategic significance lay not only in its importance for transporting oil and mineral extractions to the north, but also as a tactical barrier to the western Caucasus and a crucial junction in the rail links that resupplied Soviet (and later German) forces fighting around Stalingrad. At this time, Rostov-on-Don measured about 12km on the east–west axis and 6km north–south, with almost all of the industrial buildings and the civilian habitations north of the river.

Prior to the German attack in July 1942, Rostov-on-Don had been heavily fortified with defensive works. Inner and outer concentric defensive rings had been dug, consisting of concealed anti-tank ditches and obstacles plus extensive Red Army firing positions. Minor rivers laced the city and the northern approaches, and the bridges over them were rigged with explosives, ready for demolitions. In terms of architecture, the outer suburbs consisted of scatterings of low-rise civilian housing, giving way to high-rise apartment blocks and industrial buildings around the port and inner-city areas. Wide streets offered both ease of movement to armour and infantry, but also clear fields of fire for ambushes and anti-tank gunnery.

Kradschützen (motorcycle rifle troops) of the SS-Division (mot.) *Leibstandarte SS Adolf Hitler* head towards Rostov-on-Don in 1941. During the fighting to take the city that year, the division captured more than 10,000 Soviet prisoners. (AirSeaLand/ Cody Images)

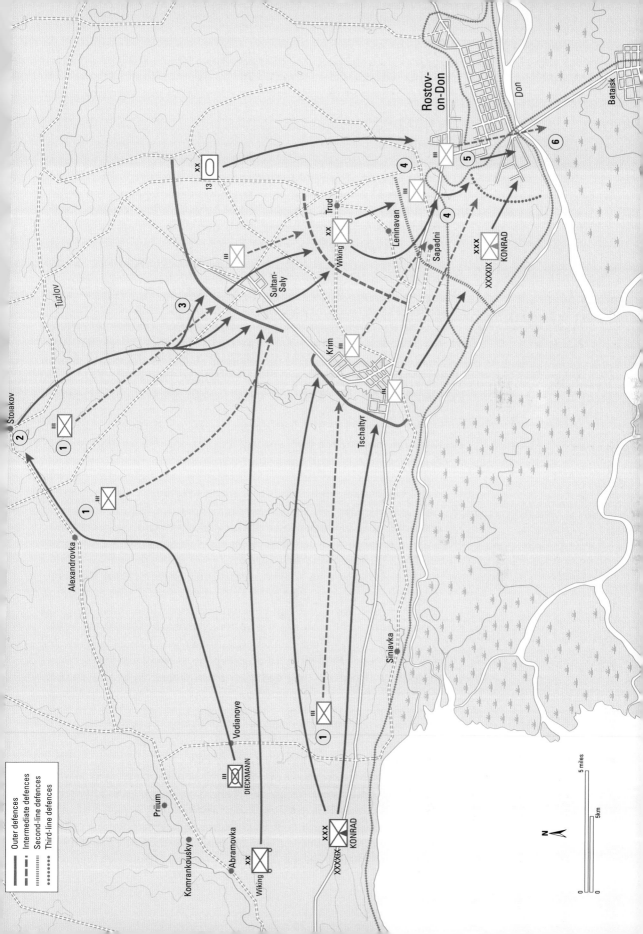

Rostov-on-Don

Bataisk

Don

Tuzlov

Stoiakov

Alexandrovka

Komrankousky

Prilum

Abramovka

Vodianoye

DIECKMANN

Wiking

KONRAD

XXXXIX

Siniavka

Tschaltyr

Krim

Sultan-
Saly

Wiking

Trud

Leninavan

Sapadni

KONRAD

XXXXIX

13

1

2

1

1

3

1

5

4

4

6

N

Outer defences
Intermediate defences
Second-line defences
Third-line defences

5 miles

5km

0

0

INTO COMBAT

Wiking rolled out towards Rostov-on-Don on 20 July, part of a general offensive movement against the city conducted by the 17. Armee and the 1. Panzerarmee. Dieckmann's *Kampfgruppe* was specifically tasked with assaulting the outer-perimeter defences to the north-east of the city, with the XXXXIX. Gebirgs-Armeekorps (Mountain Army Corps) making the drive further to the south against the defences on the eastern perimeter, while the 13. Panzer-Division framed the *Wiking* advance to the north. On 21 July, the Waffen-SS formation roughly followed the same line of advance as the mountain corps troops, tracking down the Mertvy Donets, a river that frames the south-western corner of Rostov-on-Don, intersecting with the Don River itself at the southern point of the city. Then, approximately 25km from the outer defensive lines, Kampfgruppe *Dieckmann* swung north-east, manoeuvring through the villages of Vodianoye and Alexandrovka before establishing an overnight position just to the west of Stoiakov.

The Red Army outer defensive perimeters were now only about 12km away; but Soviet infantry had also taken up positions on hilly ground just to the south of Stoiakov, and as the Waffen-SS forces moved up and through the village on the morning of 22 July the Soviet troops opened up with heavy small-arms fire. The Waffen-SS soldiers, aided by armour, quickly pushed through the resistance, but the fire intensified as the Axis troops pressed up against the outer line of defences extending around the face of Sultan-Saly. Red Army units armed with anti-tank cannon began to lay down accurate fire on the German vehicles at a range of approximately 800m, knocking out two tanks and forcing the rest of the armour to pull back a little and take cover behind some nearby hills. The German armour faced further problems when it assaulted at first light, having to negotiate a minefield, and some of its lead tanks became trapped in well-concealed anti-tank ditches. The Red Army riflemen poured counterfire on the German tanks from well-concealed fighting positions, although according to German reports the defenders seemed to waste much ammunition directing their fire against invulnerable armour. Engineers from *Wiking* and nearby Luftwaffe engineering units arrived to either bridge or destroy the anti-tank ditches, under the covering fire of the tanks, infantry small arms and Waffen-SS artillery. Dieckmann also decided to launch his troops forward in an assault. He radioed for air support, and at about 1700hrs 36 Ju 87 Stuka dive-bombers blasted the Soviet positions, adding their bombs to other fire support from ground troops. Dieckmann's men rode up fast to the suppressed enemy trenches, sitting atop the Panzers, then dismounted and managed to breach the positions. Those Red Army troops who didn't flee from their positions were killed in place during the close-quarters fighting, which lasted until about 2200hrs. Those who did survive retreated back to the second-line defences.

Dieckmann's men rested overnight in positions about 3km south of Sultan-Saly until about 0400hrs on 23 July. The intelligence the Waffen-SS possessed about the Red Army opposition in front of them stated that there was about a battalion of troops emplaced in an intermediary line between Dieckmann's group and the second main line of defences, which were located approximately 8km from the outskirts of Rostov-on-Don itself, and again

included a deep anti-tank ditch and various obstacles. The Soviet soldiers had also set up an urban stronghold position in a factory at Trud, to the north of Leninavan and just behind the intermediary line, to act as a breakwater against the German push into the city outskirts. Riflemen in heavy numbers (tens of thousands) were also on the Krim–Tschaltyr line, engaged by the XXXXIX. Gebirgs-Armeekorps, which was subsequently assisted by *Wiking* elements swinging south.

The German forces advancing eastwards towards Rostov-on-Don resumed their assault at daybreak and faced very substantial resistance all the way. The Red Army soldiers had established a robust defence. Rifleman occupied dug-in positions that provided them with good cover from enemy fire, and they also had the support of HMGs, mortars, field artillery and anti-aircraft cannon. Soviet anti-tank guns also scored hits on *Wiking* armour, disabling or destroying several tanks on the approach. Nevertheless, Dieckmann's assault troops made a successful rush attack on the intermediate defensive position, supported by HMGs and mortars, and by 0700hrs the Waffen-SS troops had moved up to Leninavan. The defensive fire coming from the settlement was blistering, however, and there was still some 800m of flat terrain to cover to make the forward assault – perfect killing ground for the Soviet soldiers.

To support the assault, Dieckmann again asked for Luftwaffe aerial bombardment, but this time the request was denied. A Luftwaffe reconnaissance aircraft, however, was able to report to Dieckmann that about 2km south of Leninavan, and 5km west of Rostov-on-Don, there was an undefended bridge that, if seized, could be used to outflank the Leninavan defences and break through the main second line with armour. While other *Wiking* forces kept the enemy busy, Dieckmann deployed two rifle companies on tanks to the south. The Axis forces made fast progress and the bridge was taken and secured at about 1200hrs. The Red Army positions at Leninavan were thus destabilized and attacked from multiple directions. *Wiking* armour surged forward against the positions and soon the tanks and armour were engaging the Soviet defenders on the final line of defences prior to entering Rostov-on-Don itself, which could now be discerned in the distance.

ABOVE LEFT
From 1942, the Waffen-SS had to accustom themselves to fighting on the defence as well as on the attack. In this photograph, a group of *SS-Panzergrenadiere* are hard at work preparing defensive slopes; as an enemy tank drove down such a slope, it would expose its vulnerable thin top armour to anti-tank weapons. (AirSeaLand/Cody Images)

ABOVE RIGHT
This image of a Waffen-SS trooper sprinting down a trench shows the effectiveness of anti-tank ditches; he passes beneath the gun barrel of a Red Army T-34 medium tank, which jammed itself into the ditch when its main gun smashed into the opposite bank. (AirSeaLand/Cody Images)

Rostov-on-Don street fighting, 23 July 1942

Troops from the SS-Division *Wiking* fight their way down a street in Rostov-on-Don, 23 July 1942. Support fire for the infantrymen is provided by a 2cm FlaK 38 gun (manned by a two-man team) from the heavy-weapons company of the III./SS-Rgt *Germania*. One of the team, the gunner, sits on the seat and directs the firing, while the other maintains ammunition supply. Although 2cm FlaK guns were designed for low- to medium-altitude anti-aircraft fire, they provided excellent support-fire capabilities for infantry, with an effective range of nearly 6,000m and a cyclical rate of fire of 120rd/min.

The gun is acting in support of a squad of grenadiers from the III./SS-Rgt *Germania*, under the leadership of an *SS-Rottenführer*, who is shouting commands for the extraction of a wounded soldier. Several of the men are armed with MP 40 SMGs, with the corresponding slender canvas magazine pouches. Note the soldier dragging his comrade to safety – as was a standard practice, he has filled a bread bag with stick grenades, for ready access to them during house-clearing operations.

On the central line of attack, the armour was decisive and made the experience of the Waffen-SS grenadiers that much more survivable – both of the available rifle battalions of the SS-Regiment *Nordland* were essentially able to advance behind the Panzers with little resistance. Both armour and infantry, however, knew better than to separate; each relied upon the other to face down the Soviet threats, which included infantry anti-armour grenades such as the RPG-40 and the PTRD-41 and PTRS-41 anti-tank rifles. The 14.5×114mm rounds fired by the anti-tank rifles were not capable of penetrating the main armour of PzKpfw III and IV medium tanks, but they could punch into engine compartments through weaker rear armour, or penetrate through the thinner plate of halftracks.

The *Wiking* commanders now had to find a route that would enable them to fight into Rostov-on-Don itself. Dieckmann and others consulted on the line of attack and decided to move south and then east, hooking around and

Red Army signallers were a critical bridge between front-line commanders and higher headquarters. A quirk of the Red Army was that even very senior commanders, up to general rank, would often go very close to the action rather than issue commands from a distant headquarters. The signallers accompanying them therefore had to be ready to fight themselves, hence the PPSh-41 SMG located close by. (AirSeaLand/Cody Images)

attacking a weak juncture between lines of defence built into the outer edges of the city, assaulting around the village of Sapadni.

The Red Army soldiers facing them were now looking at fighting a classic city defence, setting up fields of fire from buildings and street corners, finding positions from which they could launch ambushes against German troops and armour. For the *Wiking* commanders, the intelligence on what faced them was highly unclear. Red Army infantry had been detected around Sapadni, and there was a strong defensive line just south of Sapadni at Krasny Gorod, where at least 40–60 riflemen had been spotted, supported with HMGs. A third defensive line was embedded in the heart of the Rostov-on-Don itself.

The assault group for the attack through Sapadni was to be led by SS-Sturmbannführer Johannes Mühlenkamp, commander of the SS-Panzer-Abteilung *Wiking*, and consisted of one tank squadron, one rifle company and a reduced combat-engineer company, the last of these to be used for demolishing urban strongpoints and obstacles, and for removing enemy demolitions from bridges and other structures. A support group would provide suppressive fire for the assault group; it was formed from the heavy-weapons company of the III./SS-Rgt *Germania* and the III./SS-AR 5 artillery group. The heavy-weapons company, positioned on the eastern edge of Sapadni, would lay down heavy fire from machine guns, 2cm cannon, mortars and anti-tank guns while the artillery, to the south and the west, would deliver longer-range firepower from their 10.5cm and 15cm guns. A reserve group, with one rifle company, one combat-engineer platoon and one tank platoon, was kept west of Sapadni ready to exploit the attack, while a small security group was positioned further back to protect key bridges and roads.

Under shellfire (either their own or the Germans'), a Soviet PTRD anti-tank rifle team advance forward to find a suitable firing position. The PTRD was a bolt-action rifle firing a formidable 14.5×114mm round at 1,012m/sec. Its 64g bullet had the capability to penetrate 40mm of armour at 100m. (AirSeaLand/Cody Images)

Powerful artillery support became one of the defining characteristics of the Red Army's eventual success on the Eastern Front. Here we see the crew of a 76mm M1939 divisional gun taking a meal break. The M1939 was a solid performer, and the Germans put hundreds of captured guns into service as the 7.62cm FK 297(r). (AirSeaLand/Cody Images)

The Waffen-SS assault into Rostov-on-Don began in the early afternoon hours of 23 July. The return fire from the Soviet troops was ferocious, and the Panzers were held up by an anti-tank ditch while waiting for the engineers to forge crossing points. The German tanks proved especially useful for blasting out Red Army firing positions in upper windows. The soldiers of the assault group were soon engaged in the horrors of violent house-clearing, and the reserve group was committed to the action. The German attack drove forward and established all-round defensive strongpoints in the heart of the city, bringing forward the artillery so that it could deliver fire onto the Don River crossings. It was now observed that Red Army troops were fleeing across the river via its bridges and boats, and all came under accurate disrupting fire. Once the combat engineers had bridged the anti-tank ditch defences in the east of the city, the Panzers of *Wiking*, supported by Dieckmann's troops, pushed down to the banks of the Don in the south of the city, joined at nightfall by elements of the 13. Panzer-Division. They were unable to find suitable crossing points, however, so they consolidated positions while the combat engineers set about laying bridgeworks.

By the end of the day on 23 July, Rostov-on-Don was effectively in German hands. Isolated pockets of resistance remained throughout the city, some of them fiercely contested (such as the city headquarters of the NKVD), and the Waffen-SS and Heer units remained engaged for the next few days clearing these out, with some of the most stubborn neighbourhoods subjected to Luftwaffe bombing to 'encourage' their surrender.

The total *Wiking* and Soviet casualties taken during the battle for Rostov-on-Don are unclear, but it seems that the German casualties were comparatively light compared to those of the Soviets. Marini, for example, states (Marini 1980) that the combat group used in the city assault suffered just three men killed and 12 men wounded, although the total number of *Wiking* casualties would naturally be much higher. In prisoners alone, the Red Army lost *c.*10,000 men during the city battle. In many ways, the 1942 battle for Rostov-on-Don was a textbook demonstration of the Waffen-SS's mastery of tactical initiative and combined-arms manoeuvres.

The Third Battle of Kharkov

1 February–18 March 1943

BACKGROUND TO BATTLE

The outlook was truly changing for Hitler's Wehrmacht in the opening months of 1943. In the first years of the war, a major operational and strategic defeat by the Red Army was unthinkable, despite the brutality of combat on the Eastern Front. Yet by January 1943, the 6. Armee at Stalingrad was locked in the stranglehold of Soviet encirclement that began with the launch of the Operation *Uranus* counter-offensive on 19 November 1942 and ended with the German defenders' final surrender on 2 February 1943. Suddenly, the prospect of an ultimate German defeat was a real possibility.

Josef Stalin certainly thought so, and quickly looked for opportunities to exploit the perceived German weakness elsewhere, and especially in the south of the Eastern Front. Even before Stalingrad fell, the Stavka (Soviet high command) launched two major operations in the south (the Ostrogorsk–Rossoshansk and Voronezh–Kosternensk offensives) using the Voronezh, South-Western and Bryansk fronts, the beginnings of a strategic intention to push the German Heeresgruppe Mitte and Heeresgruppe Süd back to between Orel and Rostov-on-Don, punching a deep salient into the German line and breaking Wehrmacht communications to the Caucasus. The offensives had some success, creating a 400km-long breach in German lines, so planning began for the next phase to maintain the momentum.

The Stavka planned two great sweeps to the west. The first, codenamed Operation *Zvezda* (Star), targeted the area around Kharkov, including the reclamation of the Soviet Union's fourth-largest city, and was in the hands of the Voronezh Front under the command of Lieutenant-General Filipp Ivanovich Golikov. Further south, Operation *Skachok* (Gallop) aimed towards Voroshilovgrad (modern-day Luhansk, Ukraine), Donetsk and the Sea of Azov,

Soviet soldiers use a tank for shelter while they survey the battlefield. By 1943, the Red Army rifle divisions were far more integrated into planned combined-arms tactics alongside armour, artillery and air assets. (AirSeaLand/Cody Images)

led by the South-Western Front under Lieutenant-General Nikolai Fyodorovich Vatutin. Launched on 29 January and 2 February respectively, *Skachok* and *Zvezda* seemed to confirm that the Red Army was generating a possibly unbeatable momentum, driving the German forces westwards some 160km, threatening Kharkov and raising the possibility of reaching the Dnieper River.

The stars of war were already beginning to change their alignment, however, in favour of the Germans. First, the Red Army advances were becoming logistically overstretched. For example, the South-Western Front's entire fleet of road tankers was able to carry less than half the fuel required to support motorized, mechanized and armoured operations. Furthermore, the endless weeks of operations and terrible levels of casualties meant that many of the Red Army units and formations were profoundly under-strength. Looking at the rifle divisions alone, we see little correlation to authorized strength in the southern front. The 6th Red Banner Rifle Division, for example, had a strength of 9,335 men on 27 January 1943 – essentially meeting the manpower TO&E set at the end of 1942 – but the 350th Rifle Division had 6,449 men, the 267th Rifle Division 4,100 men, and the 172nd Rifle Division 3,462 men (Isaev 2017: 20); and the losses just kept mounting. There were also problems in sourcing weapons and equipment – some divisions were down to just a few dozen mortars, for example. Tactically, these weakening divisions were offering ever more vulnerable flanks as their advances stretched onwards.

Across the lines, the German forces had also suffered, and were also understrength in both the armoured and infantry divisions; but the commander of Heeresgruppe Don (redesignated Heeresgruppe Süd on 12 February), the brilliant Generalfeldmarschall Erich von Manstein, was by the end of January 1943 beginning to receive reinforcements, not least major additions from the Waffen-SS, in the form of the SS-Panzerkorps (renamed II. SS-Panzerkorps in June 1943) under the command of SS-Gruppenführer Paul Hausser.

The SS-Panzerkorps consisted of three *SS-Panzergrenadier-Divisionen*: *LSSAH*, *Das Reich* and *Totenkopf*. The three formations were veterans of the Eastern Front, and had taken punitive casualties there in 1942, following

which all were withdrawn from the front to re-form in Western Europe. They were rebuilt considerably under the new Waffen-SS *Panzergrenadier* directive of 14 October 1942, after which the three divisions received additional strength in tanks, assault guns and armoured personnel carriers. The armoured component included the new PzKpfw VI Tiger I heavy tank (albeit in small numbers), an armoured behemoth that would inflict a heavy toll of casualties on Soviet armour.

At the level of the *Panzergrenadiere*, one significant arsenal addition must be mentioned. It was at the Third Battle of Kharkov that the Waffen-SS first started to run belts of ammunition through the new MG 42 GPMG in earnest. The effect of these fast-firing battlefield scythes would be noted by both front-line infantry and high-ranking commanders; and by, of course, the many unfortunate Soviet soldiers who found themselves on the receiving end of the awful streams of tracer and lead.

The SS-Panzerkorps was not the only elite formation Manstein had at his disposal. He also had the Infanterie-Division *Grossdeutschland*, the Heer's premier fighting formation, positioned around Belgorod north of Kharkov, attempting to hold the line with the assistance of the 88. and 168. Infanterie-Divisionen. The problem for Manstein was that the fresh Waffen-SS divisions he so desperately needed were arriving piecemeal by rail and overland transport from the West, their journey harried by air attack and partisan sabotage. The challenge for Manstein was to make meaningful use of these soldiers as they arrived at the front, in what was still an unequal battle between about 160,000 Germans and 210,000 Soviet soldiers. Hitler, with his increasing emphasis on a 'not one step back' command philosophy, had also forbade that Kharkov be relinquished. It would take astonishing actions on the part of Manstein, the Heer forces and the Waffen-SS arrivals to stop the Red Army juggernaut.

Amid deep snows, Soviet riflemen jump from a T-34 as they go into the attack. The photograph perfectly encapsulates the Red Army's advances in combined-arms tactics as the war went on – the artillery hammering the target area just metres ahead, the tanks and infantry working in mutual offensive support. (AirSeaLand/Cody Images)

1 1 February: Red Army infantry and armour begin a powerful offensive thrust across more than 200km of front against Heeresgruppe Don/Süd, centring their efforts on reclaiming the city of Kharkov and the territories north and south of the city.

2 4 February: By this date, the SS-Panzerkorps is deployed in full strength around Kharkov and defensive positions west of the Donets River.

3 11 February: A limited Waffen-SS counter-offensive by a *Kampfgruppe* under SS-Oberstgruppenführer Josef 'Sepp' Dietrich inflicts heavy casualties on the 6th Guards Cavalry Corps, but fails to prevent the general collapse of the German defence around Kharkov.

4 12–14 February: A *Kampfgruppe* led by SS-Sturmbannführer Joachim Peiper begins a rescue mission to save survivors of the 320. Infanterie-Division, which had been cut off south of Kharkov. After two days of isolated fighting, the battle group successfully returns to its lines around Kharkov.

5 15 February: Kharkov is almost surrounded by Red Army forces, with eight rifle divisions, one guards division and two tank corps wrapped around the city perimeter, the only escape gap for the Germans being at the 6–9 o'clock position. Hausser orders the SS-Panzerkorps to withdraw from Kharkov and establish defensive lines to the south-west.

6 20–24 February: Manstein launches a major counter-offensive aimed at taking Kharkov. The SS-Panzergrenadier-Divisionen *Das Reich* and *Totenkopf* make a deep southern attack, capturing Pavlograd by 24 February, before hinging north towards Kharkov. Meanwhile, the SS-Panzergrenadier-Division *Wiking* in the south, alongside two Heer Panzer divisions, virtually destroys the Popov Mobile Group north of Krasnoarmeskoye. The advance north continues.

7 6 March: The Waffen-SS divisions have reached positions just to the south-west of Kharkov, the city itself garrisoned by the 62nd Guards Rifle Corps, although defence of the city is taken over by other units of the 3rd Tank Army in the coming days. On 6 March, the German forces begin their push on Kharkov, wrapping around the city from all sides and reaching the outskirts by 10 March.

8 11 March: Waffen-SS forces begin their push into Kharkov from the north (*LSSAH*) and south-west (*Das Reich*). They are confronted by heavy resistance from the defenders, who stop the onslaught in several key sectors.

9 12 March: Fierce Red Army resistance retards the progress of the Waffen-SS divisions during their advance into Kharkov. On 12 March, Generaloberst Hermann Hoth orders the diversion of the SS-Panzergrenadier-Division *Das Reich* away from the street battles.

10 15–18 March: Despite the formidable defence of Kharkov, the Red Army divisions within the city are encircled by 15 March. A fighting breakout to the west is therefore initiated (largely successfully), and by 18 March the city is entirely in German hands once more.

Battlefield environment

Kharkov's misfortunes in World War II were associated with both its industrial activities and its strategically important location. As the Soviet Union's fourth-largest city, it was home to vast manufacturing efforts, including some of the Soviet Union's major military factories, the outputs including T-34 tanks, combat aircraft, mortars, small arms and artillery tractors. It was also a critical regional communications hub, its road and rail links not only connecting all the four compass points of Ukraine. The expanses around the city included large swathes of flat steppe, punctuated by rivers (some of them wide, deep and fast-flowing) and areas of woodland and forest.

The city itself was more than 5km east to west and 3km north to south. Its town planning had been dictated by the flows of two major rivers – the Kharkov itself, which ran in from the north-east, and the Lopan that followed a meandering north–south axis. The two rivers met just to the south-west of the city centre, thus much of the city's cultural and intellectual life was contained between the rivers, with the road networks forming a roughly radial pattern out from this centre. Streets in the city tended to be wide and straight, with tall, strong buildings either side. Multiple bridges over the rivers provided defensive opportunities to channel invading forces or for slowing them down by blowing the bridges. (A 1941 map of Kharkov shows nine major bridges over the Lopan alone within the city limits.) The city's crucial railway station lay to the west beyond the protection of the rivers, the rail line running on a north–south axis. The perimeter areas of the city also featured extensive areas of open land, including parks and woodland.

The critical environmental factor, however, in the Third Battle of Kharkov was that it was still very much winter when the fighting began. The ground was covered with deep and thick snow, impairing the mobility of both men and vehicles. Temperatures touched -40 C. Although the Germans were now far better dressed for winter than they were in the winter of 1941–42, the sub-zero conditions still caused a wide range of human and mechanical problems, from respiratory conditions and reduced dexterity in handling weapons through to additional fuel consumption in vehicles and rapid battery depletion in radios.

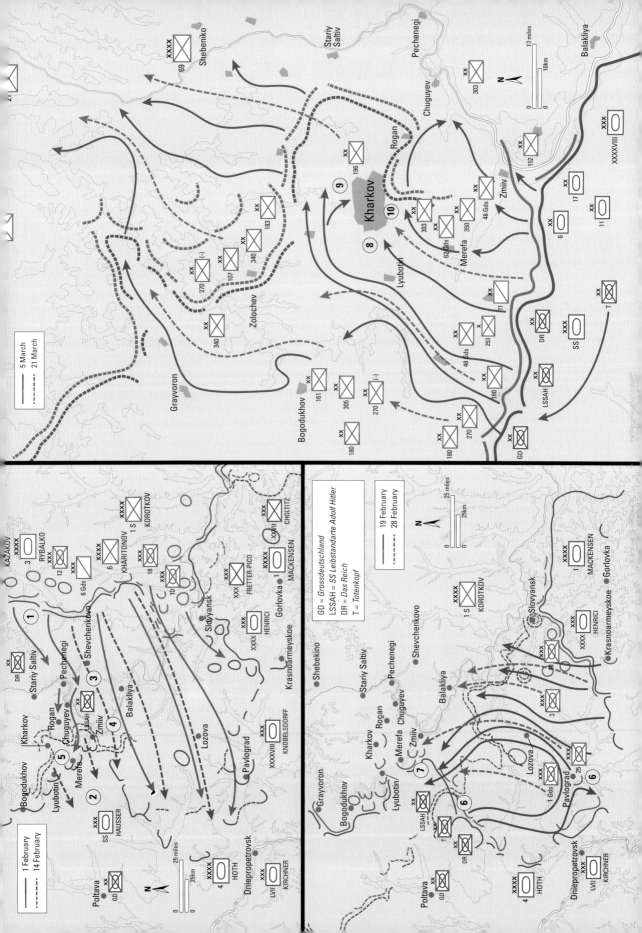

INTO COMBAT

For the first 19 days of February 1943, the Germans essentially fought a defensive battle against a Red Army with new skills and confidence, albeit weakened by the combat losses and poor logistics mentioned above. The German forces around Kharkov were pressed back by the combined might of four Soviet armies (from north to south): the 69th Army, the 3rd Tank Army, the 6th Army and the 18th Army. Holding back the Soviet tide in the south was the 1. Panzerarmee, with the XXXX. and XXXXVIII. Panzerkorps, plus the SS-Panzergrenadier-Division *Wiking*, and the 4. Panzerarmee, holding lines to the south-west of Kharkov.

As the lead units of the SS-Panzerkorps arrived at the front – specifically SS-Panzergrenadier-Regiment 1 and SS-Aufklärungs-Abteilung 1 (both *LSSAH*) and the SS-Panzergrenadier-Regiment *Deutschland* (*Das Reich*) – Manstein fed them into screening positions in and around Kharkov, with SS-Aufklärungs-Abteilung 1 extended 80km east of the city as a covering force. The Kharkov defence was soon joined by the Heer's Infanterie-Division *Grossdeutschland*, forced out of Belgorod by an irresistible Red Army push.

The Red Army forces hurled against the overstretched German Kharkov line had strength of numbers on their side. The principal formation was the 3rd Tank Army, commanded by Lieutenant-General Pavel Semyonovich Rybalko, one of the great Soviet armoured commanders of World War II. In addition to the two tank corps, a tank brigade and a tank regiment that formed the armoured heart of Rybalko's command, the 3rd Tank Army incorporated infantry formations: by the beginning of February 1943, the 3rd Tank Army had one cavalry corps and four rifle/guards rifle divisions, and over February and March the army would be reinforced by another six rifle divisions. Thus the Red Army drive on Kharkov leaned heavily on the infantry. The press on the city was bearing fruit, pushing back the Waffen-SS reconnaissance covering screen and threatening to envelop the defenders, but at signal cost. The infantry, wading through knee-deep snow, often threw themselves against the German positions in unimaginative waves, only for thousands of them to

be cut down by the Waffen-SS troops' skill with the new MG 42. (Reportedly, Hausser himself went to the front-line machine-gun positions to see the effect of the weapon in action.)

On balance, however, the Soviet troops also showed themselves capable of containing Waffen-SS counter-attacks. One such, launched on 5 February by *LSSAH*'s III./SS-PzGrenRgt 2, operating from armoured halftracks, was stopped by a defensive shield of Red Army rifle divisions, which held their ground as tenaciously as the Germans (Isaev 2017: 40). The Germans were also facing the Red Army push, led by the 6th and 1st Shock armies, south of Kharkov, threatening to separate the SS-Panzerkorps from the 1. Panzerarmee on its southern flank. A key element of this attack was the South-Western Front Mobile Group, a large combined infantry–armouir formation created by Vatutin in order to mirror the capabilities of the 3rd Tank Army further to the north. Hitler, seeing this situation develop on his maps hundreds of kilometres behind the front line, ordered a Waffen-SS counter-offensive to reconnect with the Panzer forces in the south.

The counter-offensive was launched on 11 February, led by SS-Oberstgruppenführer Josef 'Sepp' Dietrich, commander of *LSSAH*, at the head of a *Kampfgruppe* composed of motorized infantry and armour from both *LSSAH* and *Das Reich*. The attack was launched south into the flank of the 6th Guards Cavalry Corps, the soldiers and vehicles making slow headway against trenchant Red Army resistance and amid truly appalling weather. The Soviet troops were stunned by this audacious and unexpected attack, which demonstrated the Waffen-SS's strong coordination between armour and infantry, the German tanks taking out Red Army armour and strongpoints and providing cover for the mechanized infantry to surge forward and consolidate positions. Notably, when tank support was lacking the *Panzergrenadiere* found the going tougher – an infantry-only attack on Selyonie Borki by troops of the SS-Panzergrenadier-Regiment *Der Führer* was repelled after Soviet cavalry troops set up a solid base of fire using heavy and light machine guns and mortars.

While the German counter-attack enjoyed localized success and inflicted very heavy casualties on the guards cavalry, it could not stem the general

ABOVE LEFT
A Red Army rifle squad springs forward to make an assault. The Soviet rifleman became particularly adept at fighting at close quarters in urban terrain, as the buildings and the ability to move close to the enemy helped neutralize the German applications of artillery and air power. (AirSeaLand/Cody Images)

ABOVE RIGHT
A female sniper on the Eastern Front armed with a scoped SVT-40. In the pre-war Soviet Union, thousands of women had learned to handle rifles in Communist Party-sponsored shooting clubs, open to both genders, and a Central Women's School of Sniper Training was established in Vishniaki, just outside Moscow, in March 1942. (AirSeaLand/Cody Images)

Sylvester Stadler

Born in Austria on 30 December 1910, Sylvester Stadler rose to become one of the Waffen-SS's leading commanders. Initially intending to be an electrical engineer, he joined the Waffen-SS in 1933 and entered World War II as a company commander. He fought in Poland, France, the Balkans and in Operation *Barbarossa*, being wounded twice in combat and rising up the ranks. After a short spell as a tactical instructor at the SS-Junker School in Braunschweig, in March 1942 he was appointed commander of II./SS-Rgt *Der Führer* (SS-Division *Reich*) and became regimental commander in May 1943; in the intervening period he won the Knight's Cross of the Iron Cross for actions around Kharkov in the spring of 1943.

In 1944, Stadler went with *Das Reich* to Normandy, during which time troops of the I./SS-PzGrenRgt *Der Führer* under SS-Sturmbannführer Adolf Diekmann massacred 642 villagers at Oradour-sur-Glane on 10 June; Stadler began court-martial proceedings for the action, but Diekmann was killed shortly after. Stadler ended the war as the commander of the 9. SS-Panzer-Division *Hohenstaufen*, surrendering to US forces in Austria in May 1945. He died on 23 August 1995 in Augsburg-Haunstetten, Bavaria.

Red Army pressure upon the front. The Waffen-SS defence around Kharkov was both tenacious and desperate. One key action demonstrating the Waffen-SS capabilities came on 12 February, when the commander of the SS-Panzergrenadier-Regiment 2, the infamous SS-Sturmbannführer Joachim Peiper, led a rapidly improvised *Kampfgruppe* to rescue the beleaguered 320. Infanterie-Division, which had been cut off south of Kharkov by an advance of the 6th Guards Cavalry Corps. The *Kampfgruppe*, built around three companies of motorized infantry from the III./SS-PzGrenRgt 2, plus artillery assets, managed to push nearly 50km through enemy lines, load its trucks with the survivors of the 320. Infanterie-Division, and successfully return to their front lines. This was achieved despite a bridge, the SS men's primary crossing point on the Uday River, being captured and blown up, forcing them to make a hazardous re-route back to their lines, which involved some house-to-house fighting with Red Army forces in key villages.

As much as the Waffen-SS and other Axis forces could make dents in the Red Army attacks, however, the weight of the Soviet onslaught was too much to sustain, as German casualties mounted. Understanding this situation, on 15 February, and directly against Hitler's orders, Hausser pulled his troops out of Kharkov and established a defensive line further to the south. During the evacuation, fierce fighting raged on the streets of Kharkov itself, as the Red Army soldiers began to penetrate the streets and fight the German rearguards. (The first Red Army formation to break into Kharkov was the 340th Rifle Division.)

Despite this, what seemed like an indicator of impending defeat for the Germans in many ways began the turnaround for Manstein. Hitler ordered Manstein to launch a counter-offensive to retake Kharkov, and Manstein took the time to plan it properly. The plan was essentially for *LSSAH* to remain in place to the south-west of Kharkov, conducting an aggressive defence – 'aggressive' in the sense of launching outward localized counter-offensives to destabilize the Soviets. Meanwhile, *Das Reich* and the newly arrived SS-Panzergrenadier-Division *Totenkopf* would make a deep south-westward drive into the flank of the Soviet 6th Army, while the 4. Panzerarmee's XXXXVIII. Panzerkorps would assault from the south, the two attacks

Aleksei Ivanovich Baksov

During the Third Battle of Kharkov, the 160th Rifle Division was led by Colonel Aleksei Ivanovich Baksov, who proved to be one of the more capable commanders of Red Army forces during World War II. Born on 18 March 1907 in Bolshaya Kamyshinka, Baksov was conscripted into the Soviet forces in 1926, at first serving with NKVD units and rising, by May 1939, to be deputy chief of an NKVD industrial directorate. With the onset of war with Germany in 1941, however, he became an air-defence commander in Moscow then, in June 1942, deputy commander of the 160th Rifle Division, which served on many fronts. His leadership of the 160th Rifle Division at Kharkov (he replaced the wounded divisional commander) was recognized as particularly praiseworthy, resulting in the award of the Order of the Red Banner.

In June 1943, Baksov took command of the 67th Guards Rifle Division, which fought in the battle of Kursk and the Fourth Battle of Kharkov; during this time, he was awarded the Hero of the Soviet Union for his leadership at Kursk. For the remainder of the war Baksov commanded the 2nd Guards Rifle Corps, ending the conflict on the Leningrad Front. He died in Moscow on 26 November 1986.

forming a pincer aimed at cutting out the deep salient achieved by the Soviet 6th Army.

On the Soviet side, this attack would come at the worst possible time. Many of the Red Army rifle and tank divisions were down to fractions of their authorized strength, and the severe problems in sourcing and delivering fuel were sapping their offensive capability.

Manstein's great counter-offensive at Kharkov, destined to become an object lesson in confident command, was launched by *Das Reich* at 0500hrs on 20 February, *Totenkopf* (still concentrating on the battlefield that day) following two days later on a parallel route. Attacking out from positions around Novomoskovsk, the Waffen-SS divisions mounted a true combined-arms assault, with heavy tank and tank-destroyer forces accompanied by mechanized and motorized infantry, heavy artillery support, and the close air support provided by the Luftwaffe, particularly Ju 87 Stuka dive-bombers. Among the Soviet forces of the 6th Army directly in the path of the offensive there was much confusion, with unhelpful orders emanating from Vatutin's headquarters. Soviet troops found themselves engaged in several major town and city battles on the approaches to Pavlograd (modern-day Pavlohrad, Ukraine), a key position in the south, which had a major concentration of forward supply depots. For example, the III./SS-PzGrenRgt *Der Führer* assaulted the town of Gubinikha on 20 February, moving the infantry in fast using Hanomag armoured personnel carriers under the fire support of assault guns and 10.5cm *Wespe* self-propelled howitzers (Isaev 2017: 87). By 0650hrs the Red Army rifle troops defending the town had been pushed out, but returned later in a vigorous counter-attack. Unfortunately for the Red Army forces, by the time they surged back the Waffen-SS troops had set up powerful fields of fire and broke up the attack. In fact, the Red Army would make numerous localized counter-attacks during the German offensive, but none was able to gain traction.

At Pavlograd, the 35th Guards Rifle Division, the 101st Guards Rifle Regiment and armour from the 1st Guards Corps set up a protective screen around the town, and at first fought off the onslaught by *Totenkopf* infantry and armour – but then *Das Reich* joined the effort and eventually overwhelmed the defence, taking Pavlograd on the 24th. At the same time, *Wiking* and the 7. and 11. Panzer-Divisionen were busy destroying much of the Popov Mobile Group north of Krasnoarmeskoye (modern-day Pokrovsk, Ukraine). Soon the Red Army forces were in general retreat north, and as the 'pincers' of the north and south advances closed up by 22 February, the Soviet 4th and 6th armies were effectively encircled to the west.

Up around Kharkov itself, *LSSAH* was also very busy, fighting multiple Red Army divisions on the approaches to the city. *LSSAH* was extremely proactive, mounting numerous local attacks as cover and distraction for what was occurring further south, while also weakening the strength of proximate Soviet units. Hausser also formed Korps Raus under Generaloberst Erhard Raus, consisting of the 320. Infanterie-Division, the Infanterie-Division *Grossdeutschland* and *Totenkopf's* SS-Schützen-Regiment *Thule* to provide offensive flank protection for the drive northwards by *Das Reich* and the rest of *Totenkopf*, seizing several towns on the immediate approaches to Kharkov in the south-west.

An important moral victory for the Soviets was achieved on 26 February when ground fire shot down a Fieseler Fi 156 *Storch* reconnaissance aircraft carrying *Totenkopf's* commander, SS-Obergruppenführer Theodor Eicke, who was killed. Demonstrating the loyalty of the Waffen-SS to their leaders, a small *Kampfgruppe* was put together to retrieve the body of this contemptible man. On 28 February, the two Waffen-SS divisions in the south turned at Pavlograd and began their advance north, heading directly for their main objective – Kharkov itself. They would be strengthened in this push by the progress of the southern German formations, including *Wiking*. The directional swing of *Das Reich* and *Totenkopf* brought further battles of encirclement for the beleaguered Red Army rifle divisions. Units such as the 244th and 106th Rifle and 35th and 267th Guards Rifle divisions found themselves compelled to make frantic all-round defences, and small groups managed to fight their way through to join the gathering retreat northwards.

Despite the efforts of the Stavka to organize defensive lines and counter-attacks – all of which either failed in their execution or failed to materialize as the front lines changed – the German noose was gradually tightening around Kharkov as February gave way to March. By 5 March, the following formations were poised between 40–60km from Kharkov's south-western and southern outskirts (from west to east): *Grossdeutschland*, *Totenkopf*, *LSSAH*, *Das Reich*, the 6. Panzerarmee and the 17. Panzerarmee. Their main opponents across the front line were the 48th Guards, the 184th, 160th and 350th Rifle divisions, the 195th and 179th Tank brigades and the 6th Guards Cavalry Corps (Isaev 2017: 109). Kharkov itself was garrisoned by the 62nd Guards Rifle Corps, which had built numerous rings of defences in and around the city, including anti-tank ditches, street obstacles and emplacements for guns with good fields of fire along the wide city streets.

The German push on Kharkov began in earnest on 6 March. It was not going to be easy going for the Waffen-SS divisions, as they had sustained severe casualties in both men and armour since the offensive start of the offensive in February; of the Waffen-SS divisions, *Totenkopf* was in the best shape, but even that division had experienced about 50 per cent casualties in both men and armour. The plan to take Kharkov was one of encirclement

and envelopment. The Infanterie-Division *Grossdeutschland* would drive north past the city on the western side, seeking to destabilize Soviet counter-attack forces. The three divisions of the SS-Panzerkorps would also advance to the west of the city, but then hook around the northern outskirts while the XXXXVIII. Panzerkorps would advance on the city from the south and move along from the south-east. From left to right of the advance, the order of the divisions was to be *Totenkopf* (moving up from the SS corps boundary with the XXXXVIII. Panzerkorps), *LSSAH* and *Das Reich*. Essentially, the aim was to cut off and divide the city's defences, rather than attempt to seize it in a prolonged urban battle.

There was much hard fighting on the approaches to and outskirts of Kharkov. Around the town of Valki, for example, the troops of SS-Sturmbannführer Kurt 'Panzer' Meyer's SS-Aufklärungs-Abteilung 1 (*LSSAH*) had to help the division's Tiger I heavy tanks overcome a deeply emplaced 'Pak front' of anti-tank defences, defended by riflemen with mobile support from T-34 medium tanks. *Totenkopf*, sandwiched between *Grossdeutschland* to its left and *LSSAH* to its right, faced trenchant resistance from Red Army formations such as the 160th Rifle Division, which was fighting hard to retain the defensive positions it had etched into the earth. Both *Totenkopf* and *LSSAH* engaged in heavy street fighting to clear the town of Dergachi, 16km to the north-west of Kharkov. By 10 March, advance units of *LSSAH* and *Das Reich* were touching on the northern and south-western outskirts, respectively, of Kharkov itself.

Inside Kharkov, the Red Army infantry were preparing to make their stand. Snipers were positioned in elevated positions and amid piles of rubble on wasteland and street corners. DShK HMGs were positioned with good fields of fire along the broad main streets running through the centre of the city, down which the enemy Panzers and infantry would surely come. Groups of infantry also gathered in support of anti-tank gun positions. The Soviet defences included significant numbers of T-34 medium tanks to act as mobile heavy fire support. Given the nature of the retreating Soviet front, however,

A Red Army infantry squad make an attack under the covering fire provided by the DP gunner, here accompanied by his assistant gunner. Note how the LMG is placed in a sled that could be pulled over the snowy ground. We tend to see this mostly in the case of heavier machine guns such as the PM M1910, as the DP was light enough to be carried, and even fired, on the assault. (AirSeaLand/Cody Images)

The battle for Kharkov, March 1943

German view: Part of a *Kampfgruppe* of the SS-Panzergrenadier-Division *Leibstandarte SS Adolf Hitler* moving into Kharkov in early March 1943, a PzKpfw IV Ausf G rounding a street corner comes under fire from a Red Army anti-tank team about 200m away, the shell exploding in front of the vehicle. The accompanying *Panzergrenadiere* have dismounted from their SdKfz 251 halftrack and move forward to provide tactical support; it is imperative that they put down suppressive fire on the enemy strongpoint, so to the left of the scene a two-man MG 42 GPMG team is sending out rapid fire, covering the German soldiers as they move forward on the attack. The Waffen SS soldiers are wearing a mix of outer clothing items. Some are still in the winter reversible smocks, the white side presented outwards, while several of the men are wearing the insulated three-quarter length winter parka/anorak. This was a fur-lined, pull-over design (later variants had full-length button fastenings) first issued in late 1940, but distributed in greater volumes to the Eastern Front from January 1943.

Soviet view: A group of Soviet riflemen from the Red Army's 305th Rifle Division, in covered positions in rubble, open fire on the Waffen-SS troops and armour from a prepared defensive position. The bank of rubble provides decent cover against small-arms fire, but if their position is threatened they can melt quickly into the tall apartment blocks either side of them, the thick walls, multiple floors and many rooms of which were something of a nightmare for the Germans to clear. The riflemen open fire with a variety of standard small arms – Mosin-Nagant rifles, PPSh-41 SMGs and a DP LMG – and they act in support of a 45mm M42 anti-tank gun and crew, firing over a mound of rubble to the right and targeting the PzKpfw IV. If they have fire discipline, the soldiers will avoid directing any small-arms fire against the armoured vehicles, instead targeting the now-dismounted German infantry.

and the fact that the primary builder of the city's defences – the 62nd Guards Rifle Division – was withdrawn from the city itself and positioned on the south-west approaches, the internal defensive communications left much to be desired, despite the fact that the city's defence had been centralized under the command of Lieutenant-General Dmitry Timofeyevich Kozlov, previously celebrated for his defence of the Crimea.

From the north of Kharkov, the first penetrating attacks were begun by three *Kampfgruppen* formed from *LSSAH*: two of them, based around the SS-Panzergrenadier-Regimenter 1 and 2 respectively, would attack directly into the heart of the city from the north, down its main streets, while a third was formed from Meyer's SS-Aufklärungs-Abteilung 1 and one of the Panzer battalions (Ripley 2014). It is often reported that it was Hausser's choice to take the Waffen-SS troops into the city's streets, against higher orders from Generaloberst Hermann Hoth, commander of the 4. Panzerarmee. Historians such as Alexei Isaev have shown this to be untrue: Hausser was rather simply interpreting orders, and Hoth was aware of his intentions and did not initially countermand them (Isaev 2017: 116).

The Red Army defenders resisted the Waffen-SS spearheads with everything they had. Every building and street was a kill zone for the advancing enemy, the Soviet riflemen engaging the Waffen-SS troops at close range with small arms and explosives, supporting the heavier fire of the anti-tank guns and working alongside street-corner counter-attacks by T-34s. The Waffen-SS utilized Panzer and tank-destroyer gunfire to support their infantry advances, the *Panzergrenadiere* moving up close behind the tanks in halftracks then dismounting and moving behind them as the halftracks were used as mobile pillboxes. The Waffen-SS tanks, halftracks and infantry would form themselves into individual assault groups, taking out specific blocks of buildings and clearing streets in systematic fashion, one at a time.

It was hard going for the Germans, not least because fuel was running perilously low, threatening their mobility. Units of *LSSAH* were compelled to make withdrawals, despite penetrating to the central city square at one point, and Meyer's *Kampfgruppe* found itself temporarily cut off and forced to establish an all-round defence in a cemetery, later rescued by a *Kampfgruppe* under the command of Peiper. The strength of the resistance within the city caused Hoth to reflect on what was happening, and he ordered that *Das Reich* be extracted from the street battles and replaced by *Totenkopf*, with *Das Reich* manoeuvring around the north of the city, although this extraction took time. *LSSAH*, meanwhile, continued blasting its way through the streets.

It was the fighting outside the city, not within its streets, that decided the outcome of the battle. Despite pouring reinforcements into the theatre, the Stavka found that by 15 March Kharkov was encircled. On 15 March, therefore, the commander of the 3rd Tank Army began issuing orders for a fighting withdrawal from the city. With the 62nd Guards Rifle Division acting as a covering force, the 303rd and 305th Rifle divisions and an NKVD brigade were the first to break out, followed by the 19th, 104th and 253rd Rifle divisions and the 86th and 109th Tank brigades (Isaev 2017: 122). By 18 March, Kharkov in its entirety was in German hands, and the Waffen-SS and Heer were celebrating what proved to be one of their last significant victories of World War II.

The Fourth Battle of Kharkov

6–11 August 1943

BACKGROUND TO BATTLE

The German capture of Kharkov in the spring of 1943 was a final high point for the Waffen-SS divisions; but looking at Manstein's achievements in their broader context, there was little to celebrate. A pattern was emerging on the Eastern Front, in which the German forces exerted localized tactical advantage in many battles, through superior fire-and-manoeuvre and better infantry–armour coordination than the Soviet forces, but were steadily losing the war at the strategic level, through unsustainable losses and a Red Army that was now increasingly learning how to go on the offensive.

Nowhere is this mismatch between the tactical and the strategic revealed more vividly than during Operation *Zitadelle* (5–16 July 1943, although the battle itself lasted until 23 August), Hitler's epic effort to destroy the Voronezh and Central Front armies in the deep salient bulging around and west of the city of Kursk. The battle of Kursk was a titanic land battle, a cauldron of 2 million men, 6,000 tanks and 4,000 aircraft. The Waffen-SS divisions of the II. SS-Panzerkorps were, characteristically, thrown into the heart of the clash, used as a spearhead for the 4. Panzerarmee in the southern arm of the pincer battle. In almost every clash, the Waffen-SS *Panzergrenadiere* and armour disproportionately outclassed their opponents, inflicting profound losses on the enemy and advancing up to the Psel River, 60km from their start lines. Kursk, however, would ultimately only add to Hitler's now-growing list of strategic failures. The German offensive weakened after forces were diverted off to deal with flank threats, and although the Red Army had suffered truly stunning losses at Kursk – more than 850,000 human casualties and thousands of vehicles destroyed or severely damaged – the infantry and armour divisions thereafter demonstrated an astonishing ability to re-form,

In the spring of 1943, Soviet soldiers ready themselves to face a German attack. Their improvised camouflage is excellent, even flowing in the same direction as the stick shelter next to them. As a general rule, it was found that soldiers from rural areas had superior field craft compared to those conscripted from the cities. (AirSeaLand/Cody Images)

re-equip and return to the offensive, something the steadily weakening Wehrmacht became increasingly unable to do.

The Waffen-SS divisions had taken severe losses at Kursk, but they remained both operational and formidable. What truly depleted their strength was their continual committal to endless fighting, going from the Kursk battlegrounds to trying to counteract Red Army offensives on the Mius River. During these clashes, *Totenkopf* and *Das Reich* threw themselves against deep, well-prepared Red Army defensive positions on high ground, the Soviet riflemen and anti-tank gunners demonstrating real expertise in blending their fighting positions with the surrounding landscape, and holding these positions with unwavering tenacity. The costs were profound. For example, in just four days of fighting on the Mius bridgehead, *Totenkopf* lost 1,458 men, more than double the casualties it took during Operation *Zitadelle* itself. *Das Reich* had taken 2,811 casualties between 1 July and 1 August and *LSSAH* took 2,750. In return, on the Mius alone the Waffen-SS had inflicted more than 50,000 casualties on the enemy, as well as destroying or capturing 730 tanks, 703 artillery pieces and 398 mortars (Nipe 2012).

In the long term, however, German losses were less sustainable than Soviet losses. Furthermore, there were redeployments. With the conclusion of fighting on the Mius, *Das Reich* and *Totenkopf* were pulled back behind the front, but *LSSAH* was sent to Italy along with the headquarters units of the II. SS-Panzerkorps; this corps now ceased to be an umbrella organization for the Waffen-SS units on the Eastern Front. In the southern sector of the Eastern Front, *Das Reich* and *Totenkopf* – now operating under the III. SS-Panzerkorps in the Bogodukhov (modern-day Bogudukhiv, Ukraine) sector – remained alongside *Wiking* in an unenviable fire-fighting role, waiting for the next inevitable Soviet offensive.

They would not have to wait long. On 3 August, the Red Army launched Operation *Rumyantsev*, named after the 18th-century Russian Field Marshal

Pyotr Alexandrovich Rumyantsev. Its launch delayed by the struggle at Kursk, Operation *Rumyantsev* was a plan to hurl the Voronezh and Steppe fronts on a south-western axis towards the Sea of Azov, taking Belgorod and Kharkov in the process and defeating the 4. Panzerarmee and Armee-Abteilung Kempf (previously Armee-Abteilung Lanz), which together formed key components of Manstein's Heeresgruppe Süd. Malinovsky's South-West Front would provide further striking power from the east, across the Donets River. The attack became known to Western historians as the Belgorod–Kharkov Offensive, but also the Fourth Battle of Kharkov.

The Red Army formations gathered for the operation were substantially greater than those of the German forces opposite – some 12 armies containing more than 1 million men, 2,418 tanks and more than 13,600 guns and rocket launchers. The withered German forces in the region, by contrast, had about 200,000 men and 237 tanks and assault guns. The bulk of the Red Army formations were rifle and guards rifle divisions.

Operation *Rumyantsev* took the German forces largely by surprise; the Soviet practice of *maskirovka* (deception – hiding operations) was paying off. The sector of the front line between Belgorod and Tomarovka, held by just five bruised and weakened German infantry divisions, was quickly overrun by troops of the 6th Guards Army, 5th Guards Army and 53rd Army, spearheaded by more than 500 tanks, but backed by another 1,100 tanks of the 1st Tank Army and 5th Guards Tank Army. The German forces facing the attack had about 90 tanks available across the front.

The results were predictable. In the wake of a crushing artillery barrage (the Soviets had amassed more than 100 pieces of tube artillery per kilometre of front), the Soviet infantry and armour broke like a tsunami over the

German lines. The infantry worked closely in tandem with sappers, who cleared minefields and obstacles, while heavy close air support from Il-2 Shturmovik ground-attack aircraft kept German positions and columns under constant threat or attack.

In the first day alone, the Soviet operation made penetrations of up to 15km and the Belgorod–Tomarovka road was cut. The next day, despite counter-attack efforts, the German forces were unable to arrest the forward momentum of the Soviet columns, which were threatening to split the 4. Panzerarmee from Armee-Abteilung Kempf. It also looked likely that the Red Army could perform an encirclement operation around Tomarovka. The soldiers of five rifle divisions attempting to take Belgorod came up against greater German resistance, however, not least when attempting to cross the Donets River to the south of the city. Nevertheless, by the end of 5 August Belgorod was in Soviet hands, having been surrounded by movements from the east and south-west.

Other key positions quickly fell to the Soviet advance. The Germans abandoned Tomarovka and Khotmyzhsk on 6 August, and made a desperate fighting retreat from Borisovka the next day. The Red Army riflemen were now highly mobile, riding fast on tanks or in trucks to get ahead of the German capability to respond and coordinate a defence and counter-attack. The city of Bogodukhov, 50km to the west of Kharkov, was now in the Red Army's sights – but it was at this point that the Waffen-SS divisions intervened.

The Fourth Battle of Kharkov was a complex engagement fought over a wide area, most of it at a distance from the city of Kharkov itself. To give a more manageable focus on the clash between the Waffen-SS and the Red Army rifleman, here we will concentrate principally on the actions fought west of Kharkov between 6 and 11 August, when the mass of the Soviet Operation *Rumyantsev* forces first ran headlong into the defences and counter-attacks of the III. SS-Panzercorps and attempted to reach and cross the Merchik River.

Russia and Ukraine are both lands interlaced with numerous river networks, which created both defensive barriers and obstacles to movement for both armies. Soviet combat engineers became adept at bridging them, as is evident in this pontoon structure in 1943. (AirSeaLand/Cody Images)

MAP KEY

1 6 August: Red Army infantry and armour of the 3rd Mechanized Corps begin a major attack from the north towards Olshany, but their advance is arrested by the resistance and localized counter-attacks from elements of the SS-Panzergrenadier-Division *Das Reich*.

2 8 August: Red Army infantry and armour of the 31st Tank Corps attempt to push *Das Reich* forces out of positions in Zapovka and nearby hill defences, but fail to make headway and take heavy losses.

3 9 August: *Totenkopf* troops conduct a dogged defence around Alexandrovka against the 112th Tank Brigade. Murafa is captured, but the Germans hold on to Alexandrovka and prevent the Red Army infantry and armour from crossing the Merchik River.

4 10–11 August: Waffen-SS reconnaissance troops of the SS-Totenkopf-Aufklärungs-Abteilung strike out to the west against a Red Army assault group from the 23rd Guards Rifle Corps attacking around Krasnokutsk. Massed Red Army infantry attacks are mown down by Waffen-SS machine-gun and artillery fire, although the German reconnaissance battalion is eventually put into retreat by continual Soviet pressure in the sector.

5 11 August: In *Das Reich*'s sector, the division holds out against a renewed Soviet advance. The Waffen-SS troops are not only committed to defending their own sector, but also have to go to the assistance of the neighbouring 3. Panzer-Division, which is suffering Red Army breakthroughs on its left flank.

6 11 August: Against *Totenkopf*, the Red Army infantry and armour of the 112th Tank Brigade once again attempt to force their way through to the Merchik, and succeed in making crossings to the south bank and establishing a bridgehead there.

Battlefield environment

The area of the battle was framed by two major rivers: the Merla to the north, running on a north-east to south-west axis, and the Merchik, a tributary of the Merla branching off to the south-east at Krasnokutsk and forming a wide fork about 30km along its length. Together the rivers formed both natural barriers for attackers and defensive opportunities for defenders.

The area was also punctuated frequently by hills, and many of these became features over which the two sides fought hard, as they provided not only good defensive outposts but also commanding views ideal for artillery observation. The landscape was also dotted with towns and villages, ranging from the sizeable city of Bogodukhov in the north (50km west of Kharkov), nestled on the Merla, down to numerous small hamlets. Adding woodlands, agricultural fields and numerous streams, and the battlefield was a complex environment for both sides. The time of year, peak summer, meant that ground conditions were good for both vehicular and foot movement.

Two men of the SS-Panzergrenadier-Division *Totenkopf* scan for enemy activity on the Eastern Front in mid-1943. The man on the right is an *SS-Untersturmführer*, the most junior of the SS commissioned-officer ranks. (AirSeaLand/Cody Images)

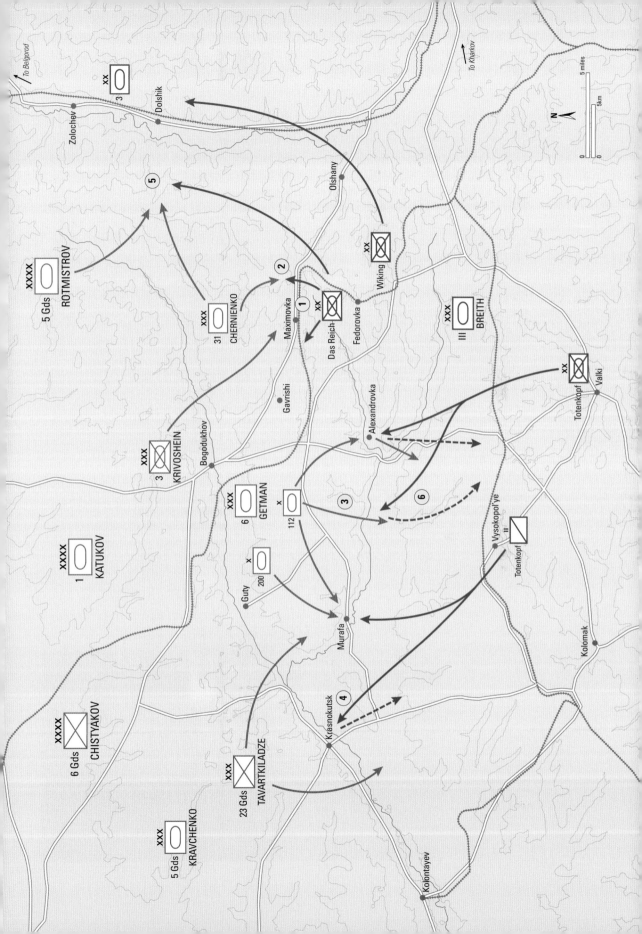

To Belgrad

To Kharkov

N

5 miles
5km
5km

xx
3
Dolshik

Zolochev

ROTMISTROV
XXXX
5 Gds

⑤

Olshany

xx
Wiking

CHERNIENKO
xxx
31

②

Maximovka
①
xx
Das Reich

Fedorovka

BREITH
xxx
III

KRIVOSHEIN
xxx
3

Bogodukhov

Gavrishi

Alexandrovka

Totenkopf
xx
Valki

KATUKOV
XXXX
1

GETMAN
xxx
6

x
112

③

⑥

Vysokopol'ye

x
200
Guty

Murafa

Totenkopf
II

CHISTYAKOV
XXXX
6 Gds

Kolomak

KRAVCHENKO
xxx
5 Gds

TAVARTKILADZE
xxx
23 Gds

④

Krasnokutsk

Kolontayev

INTO COMBAT

The first major combat between Waffen-SS soldiers and Soviet riflemen during the Fourth Battle of Kharkov occurred on 6 August, as the 1st Guards Tank Brigade, 3rd Mechanized Corps, ran into the forward lines of the SS-Panzergrenadier-Division *Das Reich* just to the north of Olshany, south-east of Bogodukhov, an important rail hub that fell easily to the Soviet forces on this day. The Waffen-SS force consisted of two battalions of *Das Reich*'s SS-Panzergrenadier-Regiment *Der Führer* plus part of the divisional reconnaissance battalion. The Soviets attacked with a mixed infantry and armour force, heavily outnumbering their opponents, but the advance shuddered to a halt against well-emplaced German lines. The Waffen-SS *Panzergrenadiere*, putting down heavy, accurate small-arms, machine-gun and mortar fire from their infantry fighting positions, withered the ranks of Red Army foot soldiers, who found themselves caught in intelligently designed crossfire, while the German anti-tank guns and few Panzers (much of *Das Reich*'s heavy firepower and armour was currently in transit towards the front at this point) knocked out numerous T-34s.

Frontal attacks on the *Das Reich* positions would continue for several more days, the Red Army troops and their senior commanders growing increasingly frustrated at their inability to break German lines they had believed would be easily overwhelmed by superior force. Time and again the Waffen-SS troops demonstrated the small-unit front-line flexibility and daring for which they were renowned, especially in the use of counter-attacks. In one incident on 7 August, Red Army troops, after repeated attacks, managed to penetrate the German lines and occupy a tactically significant hamlet. SS-Obersturmbannführer Sylvester Stadler, the commander of the SS-Panzergrenadier-Regiment *Der Führer*, immediately mounted a counter-attack, his troops fighting their way quickly into the village and ejecting the occupants in house-by-house fighting. In another incident, just eight men of 7./SS-PzGrenRgt *Der Führer* held up repeated Red Army company-strength

Red Army rifle troops head into battle in the summer of 1943. Catching a ride on a tank was not just about saving leg strength; it actually enabled the Red Army to achieve something approaching infantry–armour coordination in battle. (AirSeaLand/Cody Images)

A PzKpfw VI Tiger I heavy tank of the SS-Panzergrenadier-Division *Totenkopf*, somewhere on the Eastern Front in 1943. It was during the Third Battle of Kharkov that the division's revered commander, the malevolent and infamous SS-Obergruppenführer Theodor Eicke, former commandant of the Dachau concentration camp, was killed when the Fieseler Fi 156 *Storch* reconnaissance aircraft in which he was flying was shot down on 26 February 1943. (AirSeaLand/Cody Images)

attacks, including armour, in a small woodland area (Nipe 2012). They resisted for hours until all were finally killed, but the bodies of many Soviet soldiers littered the woodland floor. On 8 August, Soviet infantry and armour of the 31st Tank Corps made bloody attempts to push *Das Reich* troops out of Zapovka and numerous nearby hill positions, but could not make any significant headway. By 9 August, both the 3rd Mechanized Corps and the 31st Tank Corps had been unable to drive *Das Reich* from its defensive positions, and had actually lost ground to Axis counter-attacks (Nipe 2012).

By this time, *Das Reich* was not the only Waffen-SS division locking horns with the Soviet advance. On its left flank were *Totenkopf Panzergrenadiere*, defending the area around Alexandrovka (modern-day Oleksandrivka, Ukraine), while on its right were elements of *Wiking*; both divisions were engaged in thunderous meeting engagements with the Red Army forward columns. *Totenkopf* was resisting an effort by the 112th Tank Brigade to push to the south-west and make a crossing of the Merchik, with soldiers of the division holding positions at the villages of Shurvali and Alexandrovka and *Totenkopf*'s SS-Panzergrenadier-Regiment 6 *Theodor Eicke* in woodland around Olshany, with support from the SS-Panzer-Regiment *Totenkopf*. Alexandrovka itself was hit hard on the afternoon of 9 August by the 112th Tank Brigade, known as the 'Mongolian' Brigade because of its receipt of 54 new T-34 tanks in 1943, the armour funded by contributions from Mongolian citizens. Its principal infantry component was provided by the soldiers of the 112th Motorized Regiment, driven up to the front lines in trucks. The attack on the northern edge of Alexandrovka was repelled, and indeed forced back by a *Totenkopf* counter-attack, but a subsequent attack resulted in the Red Army soldiers starting to breach the outer defences and begin to establish fighting positions in the north of the town. (One reason for this temporary success was that a powerful rainstorm helped conceal their movements into the village.) Yet the *SS-Panzergrenadiere* then conducted a relentless clearance operation, finally ejecting the Red Army soldiers from their

A Soviet guard keeps watch over a batch of German prisoners taken from the battlefield. Of more than 3 million Germans taken prisoner by Soviet forces during World War II, one in three would die in captivity. (AirSeaLand/Cody Images)

new-found positions. Although *Totenkopf* was unable to prevent the nearby town of Murafa falling to the Soviets, it was able to hold on to Alexandrovka and to stop the Soviet forces from making a crossing of the Merchik.

Wiking and the 3. Panzer-Division were at this time attempting to stop the forward press of the 5th Guards Tank Army at Olshany. They were also inflicting severe punishment on the Red Army advance, but the sheer weight and pressure of the Soviet offensive was beginning to bear fruit, with a large penetration west of the *Wiking* effort. A particular problem for the Waffen-SS divisions was a severe lack of infantry personnel, their ranks having been thinned by the continual action over the previous weeks. The limited numbers of soldiers available meant that the divisions were mostly operating without any form of reserve; all their manpower was pushed up to the front line. The Red Army rifle and mechanized forces, by contrast, were taking horrifying casualties but had deep reserves of manpower, which could be fed into the battle to maintain the pressure.

On the morning of 10 August, the Soviet forces renewed their offensive across the entire front, Lieutenant-General Vatutin directing the 1st Tank Army to drive across the Merchik, push south and sever the Poltava–Kharkov railway line. Although the fighting would be hard, there would be more gains for the Red Army during 10–11 August. Knowing that the German defences were stretched thin, Soviet infantry reconnaissance troops worked constantly to identify weak boundaries and flanks, avenues for exploitation. Soon the Red Army's mobile infantry–armour teams were making deep and threatening penetrations. *Das Reich* was heavily committed in its sector, and that of the

neighbouring 3. Panzer-Division, and managed to stop multiple probing attacks mounted by Red Army infantry, armour and reconnaissance troops.

Totenkopf, meanwhile, was struggling to hold its sector against the 112th Tank Brigade, which attempted another crossing of the Merchik on the morning of 11 August. This time, fortune was with the Red Army forces. The *Totenkopf* defenders were by this time too widely distributed to present an unbreakable front, and Soviet mechanized infantry and tanks forced gaps, with a bridgehead across the Merchik established on the south bank of the river by the end of the day. In a demonstration that the Waffen-SS were still dangerous, however, a penetration of the SS-Panzergrenadier-Regiment 6 *Theodor Eicke*'s defences to the south of Pavlovo by *c*.100 infantry and three tanks was then counter-attacked furiously by SS-Sturmbannführer Kurt Launer's II./SS-PzGrenRgt 6, the battalion destroying the Red Army attackers at close quarters (Nipe 2012).

The battles for the Merchik not only showed the tenacity of the Waffen-SS in defence, but also the equally determined single-mindedness of Soviet infantry in the assault. One particular engagement, with which we shall end

Two Waffen-SS soldiers fighting at Kharkov in 1943 atop a 7.5cm PaK 40/3 auf Panzerkampfwagen 38(t) Ausf H. One soldier is attempting to fit a 50-round snail drum to his MG 34 GPMG while his comrade – unusually, for the times, wearing hearing protection – lays down fire from a captured PPSh-41 SMG. (AirSeaLand/Cody Images)

this section of the book, occurred during the attempted crossing of the Merchik at Murafa, about 15km to the west of Alexandrovka, by the 200th Tank Brigade. The principal objective of the brigade's infantry and armour was a key bridge in the village. Reasonably assuming that the Germans would have the bridge wired for demolition, the Soviet commanders knew that they had to move fast, getting troops onto the bridge as quickly as possible.

The attack was launched using multiple T-34s, each crowded with infantry armed with PPSh-41 SMGs. The tanks burst out of covered positions in the nearby village of Kosijevka and rode as fast as they could towards the bridge, which they reached in a matter of minutes. The infantry immediately dismounted, under covering tank-gun and machine-gun fire, and began engaging the surprised German defenders at close range while Red Army combat engineers attempted to find and disconnect the charges. Responding fast to the situation, nearby Waffen-SS reconnaissance troops quickly moved into the attack, killing or pushing back the Red Army infantry and combat engineers on the bridge. This done, they gained a window of opportunity to fuse the demolition charges once more and blow the bridge.

The bridge collapsed into the river, but it was a shallow and narrow waterway and enough of the bridge superstructure lay above the waterline to provide an improvised crossing for the Red Army infantry, who now began to clamber across under heavy fire from the Waffen-SS troopers on the southern bank. Incredibly, enough of the Soviet soldiers made it across to establish a fragile bridgehead, one that steadily became stronger as reinforcements trickled across and emplaced more defendable lines. (The Germans were frequently impressed at the speed with which Soviet troops could establish bridgeheads and dig field fighting positions.) The rifleman were soon moving forward again, sending assault groups out to attack the German flanks via the cover of wheat fields bordering the river. Temporarily, the Waffen-SS troops were able to contain the bridgehead, but with others now appearing on the Merchik it was only a matter of time before the full weight of the Soviet offensive gathered momentum and swarmed across the wider battlefield.

Soviet rifle troops make an attack under the light cover of a 45mm M37 anti-tank gun. Note how the soldiers are essentially attacking in an age-old skirmish line. This open formation, with nothing in the way of fire-and-manoeuvre elements, led to heavy casualties but was tactically easy to coordinate. (AirSeaLand/Cody Images)

Analysis

At several points throughout this study, we have witnessed the qualitative distinction between the highly trained and tactically innovative Waffen-SS soldiers and the generally less sophisticated instrument that was the Red Army rifleman. I am not, of course, in any way making a distinction based on personal qualities – Waffen-SS soldiers were repeatedly awed by the raw courage and aggressive tenacity of the Soviet soldier, both in attack and defence. Yet there is no denying that in the three actions studied here, the Waffen-SS almost invariably inflicted greater casualties upon their Eastern Front opponents than they incurred, and achieved tactical successes (albeit sometimes short-lived) that were generally beyond the capabilities of equivalent Red Army units.

Dismounted Waffen-SS grenadiers consult with the crew of an SdKfz 251 halftrack command vehicle, recognizable by its distinctive overhead antenna. The Nachrichtentruppe des Heeres (Signal Corps of the Army) served both Heer and Waffen-SS formations in operating telephone and wireless networks. (AirSeaLand/Cody Images)

WAFFEN-SS – 'FIRE BRIGADE' FORCES

Some of the reasons for this inequity are outlined in 'The Opposing Sides' chapter, especially with respect to standards of training. There are other factors to apply, however. The first is that the Waffen-SS, if they had the vehicles to hand, were masters of tactical mobility. Waffen-SS *Panzergrenadiere* rode to battle in either trucks or, ideally, SdKfz 251 halftracks, which from 1941 were available in large enough numbers to transport entire battalions of troops at the same pace as the supporting armour. The infantry halftrack carried a mounted MG 34/42 GPMG for mobile suppressive fire, could transport a fully armed 12-man squad at speeds of up to 52km/h, had an open-top design that facilitated rapid mount/dismount (as well as good situational awareness) and had a reasonable degree of armour protection – at least enough to stop most small-arms rounds, shell splinters and even some anti-tank rifle rounds. On the offensive, the halftrack units would often ride into battle alongside heavy armour, the tanks and self-propelled guns providing a protective wedge or front while the halftrack-mounted troops prepared to dismount and destroy positions that were either retarding the progress of the armour or which the tanks had bypassed. Without armour, the halftracks could also be applied to make rapid infantry advances to key points – bridges, road intersections, enemy strongpoints, etc. – and overcome or consolidate them before the enemy could respond effectively.

In many of the engagements of 1942–43, the Waffen-SS's confidence in mechanized operations enabled them to outpace their opponents and achieve daring encirclements or breakouts. The same momentum was achieved by dismounted Waffen-SS troops also, the squads, platoons and companies often achieving fire superiority with high volumes of machine-gun and mortar fire, allowing the manoeuvre units to leapfrog forward and take control of the tempo of battle.

Waffen-SS units also demonstrated, time and time again, other advantages in the tactical domain. They were superb at mounting improvised counter-attacks at very short notice, often reversing Red Army gains through the use of composite mobile groups. The battles of Kharkov in 1943, furthermore, showed that they had equal talents in defence, creating hardened lines with intelligently laid fields of fire and traps for both men and tanks – tens of thousands of Soviet riflemen came to grief in front of these lines, despite the magnitude of their late-war advances.

What the Waffen-SS could not do, ultimately, was fight a war of attrition. The Waffen-SS divisions featured in this book remained formidable opponents of the Allies, but the cumulative manpower and equipment losses were impossible to sustain between 1943 and 1945, especially as both the Soviet Union and the Western Allies achieved absolute superiority in terms of air power,

LSSAH soldiers take a break during the fighting at Kharkov in March 1943. As can be seen, by early 1943 the days of inadequate winter clothing for the Wehrmacht and Waffen-SS were largely a thing of the past. (AirSeaLand/Cody Images)

The Waffen-SS divisions on the Eastern Front, as with the Heer, suffered from serious problems with logistical flow because of Soviet sabotage of rail lines. Here we see a German train utterly wrecked by partisan action in 1943. (AirSeaLand/Cody Images)

artillery and (at least in raw numbers) armour. The crushing weight of Soviet artillery, for example, had a significant effect on the mobility and sustainability of Waffen-SS operations on the Eastern Front. Under particularly heavy fire, the *Panzergrenadiere* might be forced to dismount from their halftracks and trucks well behind the front of advance (about 400m was common), as the Hanomags were natural magnets for Soviet anti-tank fire, while the open-top design provided little protection from field artillery and mortar plunging fire. Another significant problem for the Waffen-SS by the summer of 1943 was the steadily emerging air superiority of the Soviet Air Force; the depredations of incessant attacks by Il-2 Shturmovik aircraft on vehicles and key logistical assets, such as railway lines and rolling stock, were by late 1943 causing a significant drain on Axis front-line capability. By 1943, one-third of all front-line Soviet combat aircraft were Il-2s.

To these problems can be added the effects of infantry combat. Although the Red Army soldier was largely outclassed by his Waffen-SS counterpart, the riflemen just kept on coming, and were more than capable of putting down fire on Waffen-SS positions, especially given their increasing volumes of automatic firepower. Furthermore, over the period 1942–43 the Red Army soldier was learning to fight with greater sophistication – through hard-won experience, the tactical gap was narrowing.

SOVIET FORCES – EVOLVING TACTICS

With respect to the Red Army's infantrymen, from a tactical perspective we see significant new roads taken in the November 1942 edition of the official Soviet infantry manual, which incorporated the lessons learned from the shambolic defeats of 1941. Take this key passage, related to how commanders led on the battlefield:

2. The old Manual placed commanders, especially those of small units (sections, companies), in front of their units. In some cases they led troops into attack.

This method entailed unnecessary losses in commanders and frequently caused disorganization of combat formations.

Obviously this part of the old Manual does not correspond to the interests of our Army. [...]

The present Tactical Manual places the commanders of sections into waves. The commanders of platoons, companies, and battalions stay behind the combat formation at the posts from which they can observe their own combat formations and the enemy. (Department of Defense 1951: 3)

Here we see special attention paid to the importance of careful and, by implication, competent command-and-control at the small-unit level, avoiding heroically wasteful leadership from the front and instead espousing better tactical governance as the battle evolved. There is a concomitant shift away from the blunt instrument of frontal attacks against the face of the enemy lines to an emphasis on flexible manoeuvre:

7. Modern military operations are predominantly of manoeuvring character. This requires from commanders a high capacity for regrouping of troops before operations and throughout battle, for conducting turning movement, encircling, capturing prisoners, destroying enemy groupings.

The leading idea of battle for annihilation of the encircled enemy consists in successive splitting of their units for the purpose of condensation of small encircled groups into small spaces and annihilating them by cross machine gun and mortar fire.

8. Defense must be stubborn and active. It must be able to withstand mass attacks by tanks supported by a powerful artillery fire and attacks from the air. Defense must have antitank, antiartillery, antiaircraft capacities. It must be deep. (Department of Defense 1951: 5)

A quad Maxim anti-aircraft gun guards the skies of Kharkov. Such weapons looked ferocious, but had no capability against high-altitude bombing, being best used for shooting at strike aircraft (particularly the Ju 87 Stuka) making low-level attacks. (AirSeaLand/Cody Images)

The emphasis on the 'manoeuvring character' of operations indicates one of the most important steps forward in the Red Army's infantry combat capability, a change that began to embed itself from the Soviet counter-offensives around Stalingrad in November 1942 and was ingrained in experience by the time of the Fourth Battle of Kharkov in August 1943. A seminal change was in the relationship between infantry and armour. By this time, the Red Army had re-formed the large tank corps it had abolished in 1941, each tank corps including motorized rifle elements capable of advancing into battle alongside the tanks. Armour was certainly becoming ever more important as a decisive element in battle outcomes, particularly as the Soviets began to produce tanks in ever-greater volumes. (In 1943, the Soviets were producing about 1,300 T-34s every month.)

At a doctrinal level, Soviet commanders now recognized the central importance of effective infantry–armour coordination. The following quotation is a translation of a 1942 Red Army document entitled *Combat Techniques for Tankers*, written by a Lieutenant-Colonel E. Matveev. In the passage given, Matveev explains the proper way in which tanks and infantry should assist one another when engaged in urban fighting, one of the riskiest combat environments for both arms of service:

A tragic image of a horse-drawn Soviet supply column around Kharkov, obliterated by German artillery and air attacks. Even by 1943, both sides were still highly reliant upon horse-drawn logistics. (AirSeaLand/Cody Images)

> Acting with infantry in a populated area, the tanks destroy obstacles, enemy firing points and personnel on the streets and in buildings, covering their infantry from enemy fire with their fire and partially with their armour. [...]
>
> The battle formation of tanks will depend on the specific situation and on the nature of the settlement (the width of the streets, the nature of the buildings, etc.). Basically, tanks will operate in small groups (platoon, company), and sometimes individual tanks will operate independently. A group of machine-gunners and a sapper will be attached to each tank for joint actions until separation. If the width of the street reaches 50m or more, then one or two tanks can move ahead (submachine gunners and sappers move behind them) with the task of destroying the enemy and his firing points located in the lower floors and on the streets in shelters, as well as cover the actions of the sappers with their fire. The third tank with submachine gunners and sappers attached to it moves at a distance of 50–100m from the lead tanks and covers their actions with its fire. Moving along the street, the lead tanks conduct observation and fire: the right one forward and to the left, the left one forward and to the right, thereby covering each other with their fire. [...]
>
> Tanks, submachine gunners, sappers and anti-tank guns must help each other on the streets as long as there is even the slightest danger. The success of tank operations in a populated area will be ensured if all branches of the armed forces act in concert in battle. (Matveev 1942)

The integration between armour and infantry here is fundamental. There is a sense of implied momentum; the armour is better able to move through the streets because the infantry is clearing a way either side, while the infantry has greater flexibility of movement because it can call on the tank's heavy firepower to destroy strongpoints without extensive house clearing.

Infantry–armour coordination was poorly outlined in the battle of Rostov-on-Don in July 1942, but was particularly evident by the time of the Fourth Battle of Kharkov. It was part and parcel of the Soviet military's return to the previously discredited doctrine of 'deep battle', in which the rifle corps, fully supported by tanks, artillery and air power, provided the heart of a massive manoeuvre unit, the first echelons of attack penetrating the enemy front lines while the following echelons punched through to exploit the penetration to depth. Given the massive losses the Red Army sustained in 1943, there was evidently much still to learn; but eventually the re-born tactics would take the Red Army rifleman all the way to the streets of Berlin.

Aftermath

The battles between the Waffen-SS and the Red Army on the Merchik River were just the opening clashes of the Fourth Battle of Kharkov; but the pattern witnessed in those first days – extraordinary German resistance being ultimately overwhelmed by sheer Soviet mass and insistent penetrations of the line – would be repeated with increasing tempo over the following two weeks. On 21 August 1943, Manstein gave the order to abandon the wrecked city of Kharkov. This time, it would stay in Soviet hands.

The Waffen-SS divisions that fought on the Eastern Front in 1942–43 still had nearly two years of brutal combat ahead of them before the guns fell

In this interesting image, Soviet soldiers move past boxes of discarded German *Panzerfäuste*, plus a Faustpatrone 1 (the predecessor to the Panzerfaust 30) lying on the floor. This image was likely taken in 1944, as the German forces steadily fell back towards Germany itself, unable to stem the tide of the Soviet advance. (AirSeaLand/ Cody Images)

silent. *LSSAH* fought in Normandy and the Ardennes in 1944–45, but ended the war in Austria (via fighting against the Red Army in Hungary) with just 1,600 men and 16 tanks in March 1945. *Das Reich* also fought in Normandy, attracting eternal ignominy for its massacre of 642 civilians in the French village of Oradour-sur-Glane on 10 June 1944. Its final acts of the war were fought during 1945 in Hungary, Austria and Czechoslovakia. *Totenkopf* stayed on the Eastern Front and suffered dreadful losses (between June and October 1944 its strength collapsed by 75 per cent). *LSSAH*, *Das Reich* and *Totenkopf* were reunited, however, in *Unternehmen Frühlingserwachen* (Operation *Spring Awakening*) in western Hungary during March 1945, accompanied by the 9. SS-Panzer-Division *Hohenstaufen*. Even given the utter futility of

On 6 April 1943, SS Obersturmbannführer Hans Weiss received the Knight's Cross of the Iron Cross for actions around Kharkov as the commander of the SS-Aufklärungs-Abteilung 2, assigned to the SS-Panzergrenadier-Division *Das Reich*. (AirSeaLand/Cody Images)

the operation, the Waffen-SS and Heer divisions still managed an advance of about 30km before the offensive eventually collapsed. *Wiking* also made a last-ditch attack in March around Lake Balaton in Hungary, but was soon compelled to retreat into Hungary and Czechoslovakia.

For the Red Army divisions, however, the last two years of the war were times of victory, if bought at epic cost – even the final act, the battle of Berlin in April–May 1945, led to another 300,000 Soviet casualties. With the death of Hitler on 30 April, however, and the final German surrender on 2 May, Red Army soldiers could rightly celebrate victory in arguably the greatest conflict in human history. The survivors of the Waffen-SS, by contrast, desperately attempted to escape the fate of falling into Soviet captivity, which promised almost certain death in a frozen labour camp deep inside the country they had so clearly helped to destroy.

The influx of foreign soldiers into the Waffen-SS began as a trickle in 1940 and 1941 and became a torrent in the last two years of the war. The recruits included some surprising ethnic groups, given the Waffen-SS's ideological alignment. Here we see Cossacks of the XV. SS-Kosaken-Kavallerie-Korps. Many of the Cossacks in German service had originally been with the Heer's 1. Kosaken-Kavallerie-Division, but were transferred to the new Waffen-SS formation in 1944. (AirSeaLand/Cody Images)

UNIT ORGANIZATIONS

Waffen-SS division

In the Waffen-SS, there were distinctive differences between divisions, depending on their type and their lineage, but we can give some using the SS-Division (mot.) *Leibstandarte SS Adolf Hitler* as our example. Up until October 1942, the division consisted of a Panzer regiment, two motorized infantry regiments (Infanterie-Regiment (mot.) 2 *LSSAH* included one armoured-infantry battalion mounted in halftracks) and an artillery regiment, plus an assortment of support battalions (reconnaissance, assault gun, anti-tank, anti-aircraft, signals, etc.). From November 1942 the division became a *Panzergrenadier* division, although this change in terminology had relatively less effect on the infantry components than on the organization of support units.

Looking specifically at the *Panzergrenadier* component in 1942-43, each *Panzergrenadier* regiment consisted of three battalions, all of the regiment's battalions receiving support from individual motorcycle, combat-engineer, infantry-gun, anti-tank-gun and anti-aircraft companies. A *Panzergrenadier* battalion had a battalion headquarters (with attached signal detachment and battalion trains), three *Panzergrenadier* companies, each of three platoons, and a heavy company with assault-gun, infantry-gun and anti-tank platoons. True to the *Panzergrenadier* name, the battalion was fully mechanized, given mobility by virtue of light and heavy armoured halftracks, typically of the SdKfz 251 series. Battalion firepower was considerable. A single *Panzergrenadier* company, for example, could bring 22 machine guns, three 3.7cm infantry guns and two 8cm mortars to the battlefield.

The smallest organizational structure in the Waffen-SS was the squad, of which there were three in every platoon. The typical infantry squad in 1942 consisted of a squad leader, an assistant squad leader, a three-man machine-gun crew (gunner and two assistants) and 4–6 riflemen. In 1943, the machine-gun team was reduced to two soldiers, the third man becoming a rifleman. The *Panzergrenadier* squad differed in having two two-man machine-gun teams and mostly six riflemen, with two of the riflemen being responsible for operating infantry vehicles. Because the *Panzergrenadier* squad was larger, sometimes it included specialist roles among its men, such as a designated sniper or a rifle grenadier.

Red Army rifle division

The structure of the Red Army rifle division in July 1943 (with little change from the December 1942 regulations) was built around three rifle regiments, each composed of three infantry battalions plus specialist combat and support platoons and companies, including a signal company, pioneer platoon, SMG company, anti-tank-rifle company, anti-tank battery (76mm and 45mm guns) and mortar battery. The division also contained an artillery regiment (12 122mm, 20 76mm guns), an anti-tank battalion (12 45mm guns), a sapper battalion, a signal company and a reconnaissance company, for a total manpower of 9,380 soldiers.

The infantry battalion based on the December 1942 regulations consisted of a battalion headquarters, three rifle companies, a machine-gun company (three platoons, each with three medium machine guns), an anti-tank rifle platoon (three platoons, each with three rifles), an anti-tank platoon, a mortar company, medical platoon, trains platoon and signal company. Each of the rifle companies had a company headquarters, a medical squad, three rifle platoons, a mortar platoon and a machine-gun squad. In turn, each of the rifle platoons had four rifle squads, but here there was the distinction between 'light' and 'heavy' squads, the latter incorporating two light machine guns instead of the single weapon in the light squad.

At company level and below, it was the TO&E of December 1942 that made a significant difference to small-unit capabilities. The number of automatic weapons was increased, particularly LMGs, ideally suited for assault operations. The authorized firepower of a 46-strong infantry platoon therefore included four PPSh-41 SMGs, six LMGs, 14 semi-automatic rifles and two sniping rifles (Zaloga & Ness 2009: 24). This additional capability ensured that Red Army rifle units had the firepower to compensate, partially, for their deficiencies in tactical movement – soldiers were encouraged to fire on the move to suppress the enemy in front of them.

The Red Army also sought to enhance firepower through dedicated automatic-weapons units. The December 1942 regulations, for example, included a full submachine-gun company, which consisted of a company headquarters and three 24-man platoons entirely armed with PPSh-41 SMGs, creating an extremely potent body of fighting men best used in close-quarters urban fighting or in position assaults.

BIBLIOGRAPHY

Afiero, Massimiliano (2017). *The SS-Division Wiking in the Caucasus 1942–1943*: Sandomierz: Stratus.

Buffetaut, Yves (2018). *The 2nd SS Panzer Division Das Reich*. Philadelphia, PA: Casemate Publishers.

Clark, Alan (2000). *Barbarossa: The Russian-German Conflict 1941–1945*. London: Phoenix Press.

Department of Defense (1951). *Infantry Tactical Manual of the Red Army (1942 edition)*. Fort Leavenworth, KS: GSUSA.

Glantz, David with Jonathan M. House (2009). *To the Gates of Stalingrad: Soviet–German Combat Operations, April–August 1942*. Lawrence, KS: University of Kansas Press.

Isaev, Alexei (2017). *The End of the Gallop: The Battle for Kharkov, February–March 1943*. Solihull: Helion & Co.

Kren, George M. & Rappaport, Leon H. (1976). 'The Waffen-SS: A Social Psychological Perspective', *Armed Forces and Society* 3.1: 87–102.

Laios, Konstantinos (2022). *Waffen-SS Panzer Division at the Fourth Battle of Kharkov*. Self-published.

McNab, Chris (2009). *The SS 1923–1945: World War II Data Book*. London: Amber.

McNab, Chris (2013). *Hitler's Elite: The SS 1939–45*. Oxford: Osprey Publishing.

McNab, Chris (2019). *The Great Bear at War: The Russian and Soviet Army 1917–Present*. Oxford: Osprey Publishing.

Marini, A. (1980). *Fra Kaukasus til Leningrad: Argentina på basis af en dansk officers krigsoplevelser i SS-Division Wiking. Bind III* [From the Caucasus to Leningrad: Argentina on the basis of a Danish officer's war experiences in the SS-Division Wiking. Volume III]. English translation by Tigre, 2006. Buenos Aires: Circulo Militar.

Matveev, E. (1942). *Боевые приемы танкистов* [Combat Techniques of Tankers]. Воениздат НКО CCCP [Military Publishing House of NPO USSR]. Translation by Chris McNab.

Merridale, Catherine (2005). *Ivan's War: The Red Army 1939–45*. London: Faber & Faber.

Merridale, Catherine (2006). 'Culture, Ideology and Combat in the Red Army, 1939–45', *Journal of Contemporary History* 41.2: 305–24.

Meyer, Kurt (2005). *Grenadiers: The Story of Waffen SS General Kurt "Panzer" Meyer*. Mechanicsburg, PA: Stackpole Books.

Michael, Robert & Doerr, Karin (2002). *Nazi-Deutsch/Nazi German: An English Lexicon of the Language of the Third Reich*. Westport, CT: Greenwood Press.

Military Intelligence Service (1942). *German Military Training*. Washington, DC: War Department.

Military Intelligence Service (1943). *The German Squad in Combat*. Washington, DC: War Department.

Naud, Philippe (2012). *Kharkov 1943: A lost victory for the Panzers*. Paris: Histoire & Collections.

Nipe, George M., Jr. (2012). *Decision in the Ukraine: German Panzer Operations on the Eastern Front, Summer 1943*. Mechanicsburg, PA: Stackpole Books.

Quarrie, Bruce (1993). *Waffen-SS Soldier 1940–45*. Warrior 2. Oxford: Osprey Publishing.

Ripley, Tim (2014). *Waffen-SS: Kharkov '43*. London: Windmill/Brown Bear.

Rottman, Gordon (2007). *Soviet Rifleman 1940–45*. Warrior 123. Oxford: Osprey Publishing.

Seaton, Albert & Seaton, Joan (1986). *The Soviet Army: 1918 to the Present*. London: Bodley Head.

Tigre (2006). 'SS Wiking at Rostov – July 1942'. Feldgrau.net: https://www.feldgrau.net/forum/viewtopic.php?t=562&start=15

Tucker-Jones, Anthony (2016). *The Battle for Kharkov 1941–1943*. Barnsley: Pen & Sword.

Williamson, Gordon (2003). *The Waffen-SS (1): 1. to 5. Divisions*. Men-at-Arms 401. Oxford: Osprey Publishing.

Williamson, Gordon (2004). *The Waffen-SS (2): 6. to 10. Divisions*. Men-at-Arms 404. Oxford: Osprey Publishing.

Williamson, Gordon (2005). *Waffen-SS Handbook 1933–1945*. Stroud: Sutton Publishing.

Winchester, Charles (2000). *Ostfront: Hitler's War on Russian 1941–45*. Oxford: Osprey Publishing.

Windrow, Martin (1982). *The Waffen-SS*. Men-at-Arms 34. Oxford: Osprey Publishing.

Young, Peter, ed. (1999). *The Cassell Atlas of the Second World War*. London: Cassell.

Zaloga, Steven J. (1989). *The Red Army of the Great Patriotic War 1941–45*. Men-at-Arms 216. Oxford: Osprey Publishing.

Zaloga, Steven J. & Ness, Leland S. (2009). *Companion to the Red Army 1939–1945*. Stroud: The History Press.

INDEX